Readings from the Labyrinth

Selected Works by Daphne Marlatt

Steveston. In collaboration with Robert Minden. Vancouver: Talonbooks, 1974. 2d ed. Edmonton: Longspoon Press, 1984.

Zócalo. Toronto: Coach House Press, 1977. Collected in *Ghost Works.* Edmonton: NeWest Press, 1993.

"In the Month of Hungry Ghosts." *The Capilano Review* 16/17 (1979), 45–95. Collected in *Ghost Works.*

What Matters: Writing 1968–1970. Toronto: Coach House Press, 1980.

How Hug a Stone. Winnipeg: Turnstone Press, 1983. Collected in *Ghost Works.*

Touch to my Tongue. Edmonton: Longspoon Press, 1984. With photo-collages by Cheryl Sourkes.

MAUVE. In collaboration with Nicole Brossard. Montreal and Vancouver: NBJ and Writing, 1985.

Character / Jeu de Lettres. In collaboration with Nicole Brossard. Montreal and Vancouver: NBJ and Writing, 1986.

Ana Historic. Toronto: Coach House Press, 1988. 2d ed. Toronto: House of Anansi, 1997.

Salvage. Red Deer: Red Deer College Press, 1991.

Two Women in a Birth. In collaboration with Betsy Warland. Toronto, Montreal, New York: Guernica Press, 1994.

Taken. Toronto: House of Anansi, 1996.

Readings from
the Labyrinth
Daphne Marlatt

THE WRITER AS CRITIC: VI

General Editor ~ Smaro Kamboureli

NeWest Press · Edmonton

Canadian Cataloguing in Publication Data
Marlatt, Daphne, 1942–
  Readings from the labyrinth

  (The writer as critic series ; 6)
  Includes bibliographical references.
  ISBN 1-896300-34-0

  1. Marlatt, Daphne, 1942– I. Title. II. Series.
PS8576.A74A16 1998   C818'.5409   C998-910205-X
PR9199.3.M36A16 1998

Editor for the Press: Smaro Kamboureli
Cover and book design: Brenda Burgess
Cover photograph: Bridget MacKenzie

NeWest Press gratefully acknowledges the support of the Canada Council for the Arts for our publishing program and The Alberta Foundation for the Arts (a beneficiary of the Lottery Fund of the Government of Alberta) for its publishing program.

The Canada Council | Le Conseil des Arts
for the Arts | du Canada
since 1957 | depuis 1957

Thank you to the National Library of Canada for supplying archival material.

Every effort has been made to obtain permission for quoted materials and photographs. If there is an omission or error the author and publisher would be grateful to be so informed.

Printed and bound in Canada

NeWest Publishers Limited
Suite 310, 10359 - 82 Avenue
Edmonton, Alberta T6E 1Z9

to all the women, both inside

these pages and beyond,

whose words inspire my own

Contents

Preface

A collection of essays? series of musings? on issues of language, identity, collective membership and self-authorizing as a woman writer, lesbian feminist, poet/novelist, Anglo-Canadian once-immigrant . . . Try again. Repeated attempts to articulate the problem of naming and the inexhaustibly unnameable contradictions of a self writing her way through the cultural labyrinth she finds herself in. Does she? Find herself? Double-play and the provisional quality of language in a writing that hovers between unfolding sociopolitical implications of language use in contemporary feminist writing, and reportage on climbing semantically out of the latest definitional trench. Tracings that work towards the gap: blind corners, sudden steps/stops, breaking through walls that hide blind spots.

When Smaro Kamboureli first asked me for a collection of essays for her critical series at NeWest Press i dragged my feet. This was in 1993 and the essays (the earliest dated from 1982–1983) soon began to cover not a ten- but a fifteen-year span as i continued to write and continued to hesitate. Besides the problem of genre, there was the problem of rereading from a later perspective. Should i rewrite to reflect my current thinking? Eight years of co-editing *Tessera*, a bilingual journal of innovative feminist thought and writing, as well as occasional teaching in women's studies departments and involvement in organizing two feminist conferences and co-editing their proceedings, had given me extensive opportunity to read contemporary theory and participate in many heated discussions. I could see "my" thought being developed, refined, altered over the years, as it participated in ongoing collective discussion in a feminist community that has been actively writing, reading and publishing across the country for the last two decades.

By then, many of the essays for this collection had already been published and were being cited, even given back to me as dogma in interview questions. This ossifying of what had seemed very much in process was disturbing. For i thought of this writing not as a series of (position) papers in academic argument, but as *essais*, tries in the French sense of the word. *Essayings* even, to avoid the ossification of the noun. Attempts to read my life and the lives of women close to me in light of theoretical reading about our psycho-social conditioning as women, as lesbians, *writing*. Attempts, in a rather immediate form of writing, to read the complex interaction between cultural representation and self-representation. If i revised these attempts wouldn't i be contributing to the illusion that thought does not reflect the temporal context of its thinking?

Smaro supported, even encouraged, my desire to approach this project autobiographically. I would use journal entries and excerpts from letters around the time of writing each essay to document the ideational "background" of each. And each would be situated in the specific occasion that elicited its writing. I can't use the terms background and foreground without quotation marks. What is "background" seems as crucial to me as "foreground"—indeed, the two are as interdependent as questions seeking answers and answers resting on the questions that called them up.

Call-and-response generates its own narrative over time. What happened when i began working on the project was what inevitably happens: the making of a book as a whole with its own momentum, its own reason for being. As such, the developing narrative of this collection provides an altered context for the essays. Some of them have, consequently, been rewritten for this occasion; some have only been more rigorously copy-edited. The most extensively rewritten is "Her(e) in the Labyrinth," which bears only partial resemblance to the paper i originally gave. As for the journal entries, some are lifted straight from the handwritten pages of their years, while others have been invented, sparked by comments in unincluded entries and by memory.

The labyrinth of culture that feminists find themselves within these days seems ever more circuitous, the monsters, once located and met, resurrecting transformed around further blind corners both within and without our traversing and much-traversed selves. A labyrinthine sense seems vital here: an awareness of the ambient. Or to misread and adapt a dictionary definition: that complex sense concerned with the perception of bodily position (position vis-a-vis gender theory, say) and motion (life trajectory), mediated by (the inner ear) and stimulated by alterations in the pull of gravity (the surround at all levels) and by head movements (individual perception). Without such a folding together of what we tend to polarize as either internal or external, keeping one's balance is, to say the least, difficult work.

~ ~ ~

With gratitude to Smaro Kamboureli for her thoughtful editing on all levels, from sustained enthusiasm for the project (and much patience) to fastidious copyediting and inspired pushing to rewrite where necessary. Thanks also to Bridget MacKenzie, who endured my agonizing with good humour and offered help on many levels; to Susan Knutson, Kathy Mezei and Leila Sujir, who heard out my resistance and encouraged me to go ahead; to Liz Grieve and everyone at NeWest Press for bringing the book into being; to Linda Hoad of the National Library for research assistance with my papers; and to Pauline Butling, Betsy Warland, Press Gang Publishers and Gene Bridwell of Special Collections in the W. A. C. Bennett Library at Simon Fraser Univeristy, for help with locating photographs.

And, crucially, inestimable thanks to all those women whose work has inspired, posed questions, challenged and mothered my own. With special gratitude here to Betsy Warland, intellectual companion for much of this writing.

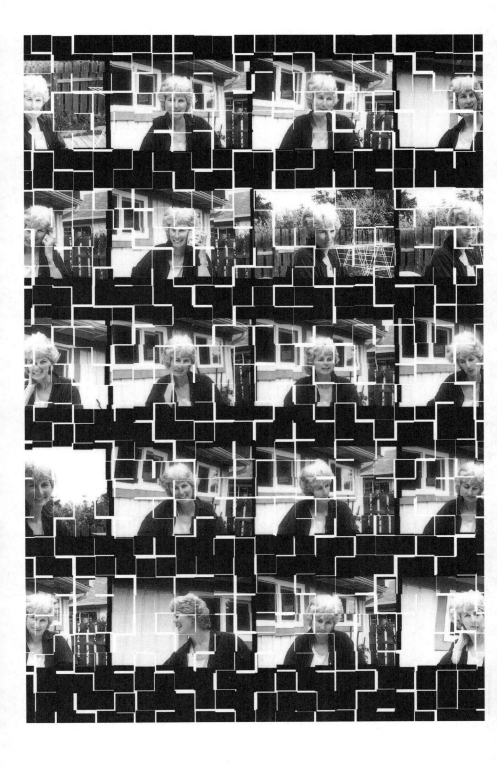

At the time of writing "Musing with Mothertongue," my first attempt to illuminate poetics with feminist theory, i was spending several months in Winnipeg as writer-in-residence at the University of Manitoba. It was a time of transition for me as i tried to integrate my feminist reading with a largely male-mentored postmodernist poetic, at the same time coming out as a lesbian in my life as well as in my writing. A few journal passages written at this intersection suggest some essential preoccupations.

Winnipeg. Sept. 20. 82

something crucial in Audre Lorde's essay on the erotic: "the erotic connection functions [in] the open and fearless underlining of my capacity for joy."

—joy, yes, one of those words i've learned to censor because it's too "emotional" or "sentimental"—i.e. "female"— but how powerful she makes it when she identifies it with "sharing deeply any pursuit with another person." "The sharing of joy, whether physical, emotional, psychic, or intellectual, forms a bridge between the sharers which can be the basis for understanding much of what is not shared between them . . ."

& then in "Transgressions" Barbara [Godard] reminds me of Nicole Brossard's focus on *le corps, les mots, l'imaginaire* —& their connections

—their interwovenness: the imaginary & its articulation of desire firing bodies once separated-off in speech, now flaming up in language/love—live with the intent to reach, to connect. . . .

~ ~ ~

Dec. 4. 82 on the train home to Vancouver from Winnipeg

reading Helen Buss's thesis on Margaret Laurence's novels, her reference to Phyllis Chesler's term "matrimony" as "that legacy of power and influence" that daughters used to receive from their mothers. where is our matrimony now? when women are "given away" by their fathers (& mothers), a broken continuity—now i see my mother's concern with passing on her jewellery was an attempt at giving us her "matrimony," all she had to give.

re-finding the daughter in the mother, the mother in the daughter—the transformative reversibility of these roles, so interchangeable— is this the drive that fuels our wanting a *women's* legacy in literature? a recognition of the interrelating matrix of women writers/readers behind Betsy's idea for such a conference [Women and Words]? a matrix that might heal the *isolation* so many women writers feel?

Briffault on language (*The Mothers*): "Thought is in fact but repressed and unuttered speech . . . to be speechless is the same thing as to be without logic, without mind." (because language is a logical system of ordering the flux of sensation/perception into a linear sentence—& can be a rational straightjacket too).

Buss counters this straightjacket with her definition of "mothertongue": "a tongue that might express [women's] deeper instincts and feelings"— how we have to break language, its syntactical rules, its labels, to convey the repressed, even the previously unthought or unthinkable—(lesbian experience, its articulation)

~ ~ ~

Galiano. April 8. 83. Dorothy Livesay's "chicken coop"

Bless Dee for lending us her place—its island-quiet so good for Betsy's recovery from the operation—each day i see more of the pain leave her face as we begin slowly, slowly to recover our pre-crisis joy

have been thinking about scripts (the opposite of gifts)—how different my script was for these 4 months compared to what has actually happened—i'd "decided" to focus as much of my energy as possible on the novel [*Ana Historic*], to finish it, decided to be only peripherally involved with Women & Words, just a member of the program committee. B. & i had decided not to live together because we'd need all our energy for our separate work commitments—neither of us foresaw her getting so ill, having major surgery, nor how essential it would be for us to live together. or that i would head up the program committee instead of writing

                    —what actually happened—its effect, rather, of deepening our intimacy & need to be together—this was what we both secretly desired. i can only think that the novel requires this living in order to be written, though that means yet *another* take, another new draft.

what *is* this strange relationship between writing & living? the novel won't get written until i know enough to write it the way it needs to be written (Cocteau's sense that the work is already "there" & the writing only a discovery of it). yet every postponement means a new draft, a re-vision in Rich's sense. exhausting—but necessary it seems. & every script i conceive for my future living is a way of "writing" my life, or trying to. of course it rarely works—or it works out on some level other than the one intended.

this twinning of life & writing, like the twinning in Phyllis's [Webb] statement for *Hug*, "it is her story & our history"—the Thai silk-weaver's shuttle volleying through the loom, catching various threads. i'm so moved by her statement because it affirms what i've felt/hoped: that anyone's story *is* an integral part of the collective (history), that it matters as such. the individual story woven around the common or warp threads (warp, its root, *wer-*, is the same as the root for *wyrd*, fate, destiny)—so the warp is what we're given in common, the threads of our collective life, what we bend & turn with the telling shuttle—& the actual weave of a life (Roy's [Kiyooka] favourite word for it is "shape") what we make of the given.

~ ~ ~

WOMEN AND WORDS
30 JUNE • 3 JULY, 1983
VANCOUVER, B.C.

Children's Literature: A326
Sexist Stereotypes
(workshop)

     Sandy Duncan, writer
     Christie Harris, writer
     Henriette Major, writer

     workshop organizer: Grazia Merler

Publishing: The Process   A425
(Two Case Studies)
(workshop)

     Shirley Neuman, Longspoon Press
     Marie-Madeleine Raoûlt, Les éditions
     de la pleine lune

     workshop organizer: Hélène Brassard

Censorship and Self-Censorship   A226
(workshop)

     Denise Boucher, playwright
     Pat Leslie, archivist
     Lorraine Weir, critic

     workshop organizer: Sarah Kennedy

Women Writers and the Short Story   A221
(workshop)

     Gail Scott, short-story writer

Writing and the Erotic   A412
(workshop)

     Gladys Hindmarch, prose writer

COFFEE BREAK

11:00 - 12:30

Inadequate Coverage of   A110
Women's News
(panel with simultaneous translation)

     Linda Briskin, media critic,
      video documentarist
     Susan Crean, freelance journalist
     Patty Gibson, *Kinesis*
     Penney Kome, freelance journalist
     Bonnie Kreps, film-maker
     Armande St-Jean, journalist

     moderator: Stéphanie Ségard

How to Improve Promotion   A104
and Distribution of Women's Books
(panel)

     Barbara Herringer, *The Radical Reviewer*
     Patti Kirk, Toronto Women's Bookstore
     Dorothy Livesay, writer
     Libby Oughton, Ragweed Press
     Mary Schendlinger, Talonbooks
     Sarah Sheard, Coach House Press
     Kate Walker, Stanton & MacDougall

     moderator: Margo Dunn

Creating Ourselves: A412
Traditions/New Directions
in Canadian Women Writers
(workshop)

     Pat Morley, critic

Professional Associations: A326
Do They Serve Women's Needs
(panel)

     Marian Engel, on The Writers' Union
     Cathy Ford, on the League of Poets
     Barbara Hehner, on the Freelance
      Editor's Association
     Eleanor Wachtel, on Canadian
      Periodical Publishers' Association
      and Periodical Writers' Association

     moderator: Sandy Duncan

Language and Language   A226
Theory in Women's Writing
(panel)

     Louky Bersianik, novelist, poet
     Louise Cotnoir, editor, critic
     Daphne Marlatt, poet, editor
     Sharon Thesen, poet, editor

     moderator: Silvia Bergersen

Native and Western Myth   A221
in Canadian Women's Writing
(workshop)

     Smaro Kamboureli, University of
      Manitoba, English
     ~~Christine Morris, University of~~
     ~~Lethbridge, Native American Studies~~

What Gets Selected and Taught   A425
(panel)

Priscilla Galloway, curriculum specialist
with Toronto Board of Education
Shirley Neuman, University of Alberta
Johanna Stuckey, editor, *Canadian
Woman Studies*, York University
Mair Verthuy, Simone de Beauvoir
Institute

moderator: Patricia Maika

LUNCH BREAK

2:00 - 3:30

When is Art Subversive?   **A110**
When Does Politics Subvert Art?
(panel with simultaneous translation)

Louise Forsyth, critic
Maxine Gadd, poet
K.O. Kanne, poet
Judith Merril, fiction writer, radio and
television writer
Madeleine Ouellette-Michalska, critic

moderator: Christianne Richards

Women's Creativity and   **A221**
Brain Research
(workshop)

Penny Kemp, poet, playwright, editor
Gerri Sinclair, freelance journalist, poet

Differences Between French and   **A226**
English Canadian Women Writers Since 1950
(panel)

Cécile Cloutier, poet
Gwladys Downes, poet and translator
✓ Barbara Godard, critic and translator
Pat Morley, critic
Thong Vuong-Riddick, critic

moderator: Anne Scott

Strategies for Change   **A104**
(panel)

Rina Fraticelli, dramaturge
Sharon Nelson, poet, editor
Sharon Pollock, playwright
Nanci Rossov, film and theatre director,
writer

moderator: Sharon Nelson

History of Feminist   **A326**
Presses and Magazines
(workshop)

Francine Pelletier, editor
Lois Pike, editor and publisher
Frances Rooney, researcher and writer

workshop organizer: Sally Ireland

Opportunities of the Long Poem   **A412**
(workshop)

Travis Lane, poet

Writing From a Native   **A425**
Woman's Perspective
(workshop)

Jeannette Armstrong, writer of
children's books
Maria Campbell, fiction writer,
playwright
Beth Cuthand, writer and journalist

COFFEE BREAK

4:00 - 5:30

Open Readings   **A110 and A104**

Short Theatre Pieces   **music recital hall**

"Les vaches de nuit"
(Joviette Marchessault) — Pol Pelletier
"The Apple in the Eye" (Margaret
Hollingsworth) — Judith Greenberg
"Integrated Circuits" (Robin Endres)
— Robin Endres and others

SUNDAY, JULY 3

9:00 - 9:45 am

Breakfast   **SUB ballroom**

Hosted by West Coast Women and Words
. Society

9:45 - 11:15

Plenary   **SUB ballroom**

CALL FOR CONTRIBUTORS: TESSERA

We are a women's editorial collective interested in publishing
feminist literary criticism in a Canadian/Quebec context. We want
to begin a continuing dialogue on women's writing with respect to
language and structure. This will take the form of special issues
in various Canadian/Quebec journals, with a projected first
appearance in A ROOM OF ONE'S OWN in mid-1983.

Editorial Collective: B. Godard, Daphne Marlatt, K. Mezei, Gail Scott

THE THEME FOR OUR FIRST ISSUE IS DUPLICITY OR DOUBLENESS IN LANGUAGE.
THIS COULD RANGE FROM TEXTUAL ANALYSIS TO STUDIES IN GENRE.   PLEASE
SEND YOUR PROPOSALS AT ONCE, YOUR CONTRIBUTIONS BY OCTOBER 30, 1982
TO:

K. Mezei, English Dept.   B. Godard, English Dept.
Simon Fraser University   York University
Burnaby, B.C. V5A 1S6   OR   4700 Keele St.
                                     Downsview, Ont. M3J 1P3

We envision a range of genres--essays, letters, interviews, discussions, exchanges, re-
flections, texts. The issues will be bilingual with synopses in the other language. We
are not interested in thematic criticism or essays that focus on content or image of
women. As a start we prefer to focus on Canadian and Quebec writing.

Musing with Mothertongue

The first draft of this essay was written during the fall of 1982 in Winnipeg when i was also writing the poems of Touch to my Tongue. *It was written in the wake of rapid changes in my thinking about my relationship to language as a woman writer. These changes had been set in motion by the Dialogue Conference that Barbara Godard organized at York University a year earlier, a conference that was for me a major turning point. It was there that i first met Betsy Warland, as well as Nicole Brossard, Louky Bersianik, Kathy Mezei, Gail Scott, Louise Cotnoir and Barbara herself, among others. Stimulated by the theoretical energy of the feminist writers from Quebec, i pursued with Kathy, Barbara and Gail our need for a journal where we could continue the dialogue between Francophone and Anglophone writers and critics.*

Then in the summer of 1983, the Women and Words/Les femmes et les mots Conference, which Betsy initiated and coordinated with Victoria Freeman and the support of a core group of women in Vancouver, brought together scores of Francophone, Anglophone, white, First Nations, Asian and Black women writers, editors, publishers, translators, critics and readers for a spirited series of discussions and performances. It was the first and largest gathering of women across the country who were active in so many different areas. It also gave Barbara (in Toronto), Kathy (in Vancouver), Gail (in Montreal) & me the opportunity to get together for our first editorial discussion about Tessera.

"Musing with Mothertongue" initially appeared, along with other texts from the conference, in our first issue (1984), a guest issue of the already well-established Room of One's Own *(Vancouver).*

the beginning: language, a living body we enter at birth, sustains and contains us. it does not stand in place of anything else, it does not replace the bodies around us. placental, our flat land, our sea, it is both place (where we are situated) and body (that contains us), that body of language we speak, our mothertongue. it bears us as we are born in it, into cognition.

language is first of all for us a body of sound. leaving the water of the mother's womb with its one dominant sound, we are born into this other body whose multiple sounds bathe our ears from the moment of our arrival. we learn the sounds before we learn what they say: a child will speak baby-talk in pitch patterns that accurately imitate the sentence patterns of her mothertongue. an adult who cannot read or write will speak his mothertongue without being able to say what a particular morpheme or even word in a phrase means. we learn nursery rhymes without understanding what they refer to. we repeat skipping songs significant for their rhythms. gradually we learn how the sounds of our language are active as meaning, and then we go on learning for the rest of our lives what the words are actually saying.

in poetry, which has evolved out of chant and song, in rhyming and tone-leading, whether they occur in prose or poetry, sound will initiate thought by a process of association. words call each other up, evoke each other, provoke each other, nudge each other into utterance. we know from dreams and schizophrenic speech how deeply association works in our psyches, a form of thought that is not rational but erotic because it works by attraction. a drawing, a pulling toward. a "liking." Germanic *lik-*, body, form; like, same.

like the atomic particles of our bodies, phonemes and syllables gravitate toward each other. they attract each other in movements we call assonance, euphony, alliteration, rhyme. they are drawn together and echo each other in rhythms we identify as feet—lines run on, phrases patter like speaking feet. on a macroscopic level, words evoke each other in movements we know as puns and figures of speech. (these endless similes, this continuing fascination with making one out of two, a new one, a simultitude.) meaning moves us deepest the more of the whole field it puts together, and so we get sense where it borders on nonsense ("what is the sense of it all?") as what we sense our way into. the sentence. ("life.") making our multiplicity whole and even intelligible by the end-point. intelligible: logos there in the gathering hand, the reading eye.

hidden in the etymology and usage of so much of our vocabulary for verbal communication (contact, sharing) is a link with the body's physicality: matter (the import of what you say) and matter and by extension mother; language and tongue; to utter and outer (give birth again); a part of speech and a part of the body; pregnant with meaning; to mouth (speak) and the mouth with which we also eat and make love; sense (meaning) and that with which we sense the world; to relate (a story) and to relate to somebody, related (carried back) with its connection with bearing (a child); intimate and to intimate; vulva and voluble; even sentence, which comes from a verb meaning to feel.

like the mother's body, language is larger than us and carries us along with it. it bears us, it births us, insofar as we bear with it. if we are poets we spend our lives discovering not just what *we* have to say but what language is saying as it carries us with it. in etymology we discover a history of verbal relations (a family tree, if you will) that has preceded us and given us the world we live in. the given, the immediately presented, as at birth—a given name a given world. we know language structures our world, and in a crucial sense we cannot see what we cannot verbalize, as the work of Whorf and ethnolinguistics has pointed out to us. here we are truly contained within the body of our mothertongue. and even the physicists, chafing at these limits, say that the glimpse physics now gives us of the nature of the universe cannot be conveyed in a language based on the absolute difference between a noun and a verb. poetry has been demonstrating this for some time.

if we are women poets, writers, speakers, we also take issue with the given, hearing the discrepancy between what our patriarchally loaded language bears (can bear) of our experience and the difference from it our experience bears out—how it misrepresents, even miscarries, and so leaves unsaid what we actually experience. can a pregnant woman be said to be "master" of the gestation process she finds herself within—is that her relationship to it? (Kristeva 238) are women included in the statement "God appearing as man"? (has God ever appeared as a woman?) can a woman ever say she is "lady of all she surveys," or could others ever say of her she "ladies it over them"?

so many terms for dominance in English are tied up with male experiencing, masculine hierarchies and differences (exclusion), patriarchal holdings with their legalities. where are the poems that celebrate the soft letting-go the flow of menstrual blood is as it leaves her body? how can the standard sentence structure of English with its linear authority, subject through verb to object, convey the wisdom of endlessly repeating and not exactly repeated cycles her body knows? or the mutuality her body shares embracing other bodies, children, friends, animals, all those she customarily holds and is held by? how can the separate nouns "mother" and "baby" convey the fusion, bleeding womb-infant mouth, she experiences in those first days of feeding? what syntax can carry the turning herself inside out in love when she is both sucking mouth and hot gush on her lover's tongue?

Julia Kristeva says: "If it is true that every national language has its own dream language and unconscious, then each of the sexes—a division so much more archaic and fundamental than the one into languages—would have its own unconscious wherein the biological and social program of the species would be ciphered in confrontation with language, exposed to its influence, but independent from it" (241). i link this with the call so many feminist writers in Quebec have issued for a language that returns us to the body, a woman's body and the largely unverbalized, presyntactic, postlexical field it knows. postlexical in that, as Mary Daly shows, with intelligence (that gathering hand) certain words (dandelion sparks) seed themselves back to original and originally related meanings. this is a field where words mutually attract each other, fused by connection, enthused (inspired) into variation (puns, word play, rhyme at all levels), fertile in proliferation (offspring, rooting back to *al-*, seed syllable to grow, and leafing forward into *alma*, nourishing, a woman's given name, soul, inhabitant.)

inhabitant of language, not master, not even mistress, this new woman writer (Alma, say) in having is had, is held by it, what she is given to say. in giving it away is given herself, on that double edge where she has always lived, between the already spoken and the unspeakable, sense and non-sense. only now she writes it, risking nonsense, chaotic language leafings, unspeakable breaches of usage, intuitive leaps. inside language she leaps for joy, shoving out the walls of taboo and propriety, kicking syntax, discovering life in old roots.

language thus speaking (i.e., inhabited) relates us, takes us back to where we are, as it relates us to the world in a living body of verbal relations. articulation: seeing the connections (and the thighbone, and the hipbone, etc.). putting the living body of language together means putting the world together, the world we live in: an act of composition, an act of birthing, us, uttered and outered there in it.

Vancouver. April 21. 83

reading Barbara's "Eccentric, Ex-centriques" essay: "Women being
displaced from the centre of our society learn the lesson of difference
on the margin"—ex-centriques, yes (& so playing <u>with</u> the literal
margin? my long line in *Steveston*?)—"Their de-centred position allows,
indeed ensures, that their gestures, language & writing will be . . .
ex-perimental":

      —off the perimeter (of print)—this vision of the
possibilities latent in the white space of the poem (why not in prose too?
space between fragments of narrative? where a jarring resonates between
various perspectives, shifts in consciousness of a single narrator or
different narrators?—white space not just inert background to print,
to what is said, but live with the unsaid, the yet-to-be-spoken, even the
unspeakable . . .

BG again: "It is in this interest in the hitherto unsaid that we find the
key to both feminist concerns & the avant-garde, & central to both is
the issue of intransigent language that has become detached from
reality"—the "intransigence" in this, that "a common tongue for both
colonizer & colonized makes it difficult for the latter to express their
unique situation" because "de-centred, considered as others, [they]
have difficulty perceiving themselves as subjects," that is as <u>speaking</u>
subjects, tho subject (to) in other ways

      —yes, that's what i want to work with,
these cross-cuttings or intersections (colonialism, feminism, otherness,
isolation & eccentricity (madness), Ina's struggle, & Annie's not to
repeat it—the public/private split—Annie's feelings of "belonging" (to
this place, Vancouver—as well as being "Canadian," what that might
mean?) cross-cut with her displacement as a woman

      —unlike her mother she
uses her immigrant experience as a way of belonging by seeing it thru a
feminist lens & fusing love-of-place with love of a woman (in the <u>body</u>,

because the body doesn't speak in systems of power, its "speaking,"
an upheaval, breaks out through the codes that repress it)

Ina: colonizer become (recognizing she's become) colonized—for her the
unbridgeable gap between these two:

> dancing to jazz on a tropical terrace
> vs. ironing sheets in a N. Van. kitchen (to opera yet!)

~ ~ ~

Entering In: The Immigrant Imagination

I was invited to participate in a panel discussion on "The Immigrant Imagination," with Sam Selvon and Michael Ondaatje, during a Canadian Association for Commonwealth Literature and Language Studies (ACLALS) session, part of the Learned Societies Conference at UBC in late May 1983. Somehow, amidst numerous committee meetings for Women and Words (which would take place a month later), packing to move house and incessant thinking about Ana Historic, *then pushed to a back burner but simmering away, this essay wrote itself. It first appeared in print in the one hundredth anniversary issue of* Canadian Literature *(spring 1984).*

The paired words immigrant and *emigrant* have always fascinated me because of the gestures implicit in their prefixes, a leaving something behind (with its backward look) and an entering into something new. The old-world nostalgia of the emigré must colour my notion of an emigrant imagination because i think of that imagination as rooted, bound up in, the place left, the "old country," "home" and preoccupied with recreating that place, whether out of nostalgia (a longing to return) or fury (that avenging spirit that cannot let go of old wounds). I think of Joyce and Garcia Marquez as two poles of the emigrant imagination.

The immigrant imagination seems to me, on the contrary, to embrace the new place it enters. It seeks to enter into its mystery, its this-ness, to penetrate it imaginatively even as it enters from outside. I think of Malcolm Lowry and Mexico, Audrey Thomas and Africa—does this mean all travel writing is writing from the immigrant imagination?

Only, i think, when it genuinely struggles to pierce the difference, the foreignness, the mystery of the new place with its other culture, as it does in these two writers.

Looking back, i think that most of my writing has been a vehicle for entry into what was for me the new place, the new world. I immigrated to Vancouver from Malaysia as a child age nine and spent many years trying so hard to assimilate, to speak and dress and behave as a West Coast Canadian, that when people asked where i came from i would say, "Oh, North Van." Though my parents' house was filled with furniture and curios and articles of clothing from Malaysia, though they both spoke with British accents and shared a common wealth of memories from Penang days with us—"remember Eng Kim? remember Camville?"—though we all wore Chinese slippers around the house (and i still do), out on the street i tried to look as much like a normal North Van kid as possible. For the sake of entry and acceptance i denied for years my history and that of my parents.

My mother came from a colonial medical family that had been in India for two generations: she was born there, as was her mother. She met my father in Malaysia, where she had joined her parents after graduating from an English boarding school. My father came from a military family, had lived as a child in India and Malta, had gone out to Malaysia as a young C.A. and, except for the war years when Malaysia was occupied by the Japanese and he was serving with the Australian navy, he spent almost twenty years in Penang before immigrating to Canada. They both referred to England as home, and yet they chose not to go home when they left Penang. I grew up with two nostalgias in our house: the nostalgia for England, which, having spent only some months there, i didn't really understand; the nostalgia for Penang, which i could share, though it was effaced by my enthusiasm for *this* place here. I loved this place, loved the woods out our back door, the Grouse Mountain streets, the dark inlet and the beckoning glitter of lights "overtown." I dreamed harbour dreams, Stanley Park dreams, Lonsdale Avenue dreams and nightmares. I wanted to "belong," to be "from" here but found there were differences not easy to bridge.

We came from a colonial multicultural situation in Penang, where five languages were spoken in our house (English, Malay, Hokkien, Tamil, Thai) to a city which was then (1951) much more monocultural than it is today, decidedly WASP, conservative and suspicious of newcomers. We spoke the same language but not the same dialect and were consequently made fun of at school. We wore different clothes, ate slightly different foods. I learned to say tomayto instead of tomahto, sweater instead of woolly, i learned to speak of catchers and basemen, to square dance, to wear nylon slips instead of woollen "vests," and learned not to bring curry tarts to school in my lunchbox. Thirty years ago, American culture hadn't infiltrated the rest of the world as it has now. When i arrived, i'd never seen baseball (i'd never even seen snow), didn't know what a parka was, or jeans, or a hamburger. I knew what orange squash was but not Mountain Dew or Dr. Pepper or Coca-Cola. I'd never heard of bubble gum or jaw-breakers or chickenbones. Here i heard country and western music for the first time and loved the stories in it. I discovered Mark Trail on cereal boxes and a completely new range of fauna and flora outdoors, from skunk cabbage to cougars. Where we lived, in the last block of a street that stopped at a ridge too steep to pave, bears periodically raided our garbage cans. I was used to wild monkeys terrorizing our chickens in the garden in Penang and bears seemed much more exotic. Yet if i talked about the monkeys or the cobras and scorpions at school, the other kids thought *that* was so exotic i must be making it up. This experience of a turning upside down of the world, an inversion of values, permeated everything. I had been taught civility, to say "excuse me" and "thank you" as an essential oil to smooth the rough edges of racial and class differences. Here it was taken as prissy overpoliteness—"why do you keep saying 'sorry' all the time?" I learned that reading historical romances like *The Scarlet Pimpernel*, or reading Keats and Tennyson (my mother's view of a basic education) taught me nothing of social use if i hadn't read Nancy Drew or heard of Bill Haley and the Comets.

So i bought rock 'n' roll 78s, put away my mother's copies of Keats and Tennyson, wore white bucks and jeans and pencil-line skirts. I loved the principles of democracy as we argued them out in school, loved Canadian history with its romance of the *couriers de bois*, the Métis uprising, Simon Fraser tracing rivers, Pauline Johnson and Emily Carr recording a culture as exotic as any Malay kampong's— and here it had something important to say about the plants and rocks and animals we lived and would go on living among. (I didn't stop, then, to question the application of "democracy" to reservations.) Wanting to sing "O Canada" along with everyone else at school (we did in those days), i enthusastically became a Canadian citizen.

Only later, years later, did i begin to feel that, like a phantom limb, part of me, that Penang past, not quite cut off, still twitched alive and wanted acknowledging. Twenty-five years after we had left Penang, i went back for a visit with my father and sister, living in the first house we had lived in as a family, sleeping in the same bedroom, finding in the amah of the house the same woman who had been our amah when we were children. This gift, this extraordinary re-enactment broke my self-taboo on the past, and i began writing about it ("The Month of Hungry Ghosts," later collected in *Ghost Works.*) Similarly, going back to England five years later sparked, in *How Hug a Stone*, some "English" writing (an attempt to capture that voice, that ethos i recognized in my parents). Yet both returns were incomplete, filtered always through my present Canadian consciousness, not truly emigrant in that what was once "home" (Penang, if not England) now seemed as irretrievably foreign as it had once been childishly familiar. My political consciousness told me very definitely that i had never and would never "belong" there.

Then, when i collected an oral history of Strathcona with Carole Itter (*Opening Doors*), I discovered how isolated my experience as an immigrant had been. Strathcona is the immigrant neighbourhood of Vancouver, has functioned as such for decades. It lies adjacent to commercial Chinatown and is now largely Chinese though it was once known as Little Italy, was home to the first Jewish settlement and before the war had a school population that was sixty per cent Japanese. I lived in it for six years and felt completely at home, felt as if part of me had been returned to a whole i'm still discovering. But what astonished me was how collective the immigrant experience was amongst the people we interviewed, whether they were Japanese, Chinese, Italian, Yugoslavian or Jewish. Most immigrant children seemed to have grown up in extended families formed by the phenomenon of "calling over," where one member immigrates and then gradually calls over other members of his extended family to the new country. In addition, there were numerous regional associations, from the Chinese tong or clan houses to the Italian district groups. All of this helped keep the original culture alive by celebrating festivals in traditional ways and gathering people together with traditional rituals at weddings, christenings, funerals, etc.

I can only remember one family we knew who had a similar background to ours, and they ended up moving to Toronto. We children made friends at school, my father made friends at the office, my mother, at home all the time, was more isolated. There were no relatives living a few blocks away. There were no neighbours to chat with who might have come from the same district in the old country, even the same town. In fact, my mother had no district in England her family could be said to come from.

So the nostalgia for England (where her parents had retired) and for Penang increased at home as our assimilation, as children, developed outside in the neighbourhood and at school. As we struggled very hard to become Canadian, my mother tried to keep us "English" in our behaviour and values. This led to a deepening rift i could neither understand nor address, as it only increased my determination to leave all that behind and completely enter into this new place here.

It seems to me that the situation of being such an immigrant is a perfect seed-bed for the writing sensibility. If you don't belong, you can *imagine* you belong, you can retell its history in a way that admits you (as I did in *Vancouver Poems*). Or you can register your presence in a world you are drawn to (*Steveston*), even as, from outside it, you witness its specific and other characteristics. It now seems oddly indicative that my first piece of published writing was a sketch i wrote in school in the first person as Gassy Jack reminiscing at the end of his life on the growth of Gastown. It was published in a local Parent-

Teacher Association magazine, no doubt as an example of student absorption of history, but what i was trying to do was write my way into a city i wanted to belong in and felt i didn't, quite.

The sensation of having your world turned upside down or inverted also, i think, leads to a sense of the relativity of both language and reality as much as it leads to a curiosity about other people's realities (the kind of curiosity that makes you wander by lit rooms at night and invent characters who live in them—a basic fictional urge). It leads to an interest in and curiosity about language, a sense of how language shapes the reality you live in, an understanding of how language is both idiosyncratic (private) and shared (public), and the essential duplicity of language, its capacity to mean several things at once, its figurative or transformational powers. When you are told, for instance, that what you call earth is really dirt, or what you have always called the woods (with English streams) is in fact the bush (with its creeks), you experience the first split between name and thing, signifier and signified, and you take that first step into a linguistic world that lies adjacent to but is not the same as the world of things and indeed operates on its own linguistic laws.

The sensation of living in *this* place with its real people and things, of being contained in it but knowing that somewhere else there exists *that* place, with its real people and things which you can no longer return to, although they are both somehow you, produces a desire to fuse the two places, the two (at least) selves. Perhaps writers who feel this way are often interested in myth and symbol because these are common to disparate phenomena and form a universal language underlying the specifics of the local—at any rate, earlier Canadian literature is full of myth and symbol. As a member of a subsequent writing generation, i'm more interested in focussing the immediate, shifting the experience of distance and dislocation through the use of montage, juxtaposition, superimposing disparate and specific images from several times and places. I want to see the world as multidimensional as possible and ourselves present within it.

have been retyping & editing the *Tessera* transcript of our editorial discussion ["SP/ELLE"]—all this talk of matrix—how the textual matrix generates new meanings because, in contrast to a criticism built on quotation, which Barbara describes as distanced (under the banner of being "objective"), the new theoretical writing we're looking for is closer, more subjective, rises from within the ongoing body of women's texts. particularly within the body of any text it alludes to, by using the language of that other text to further its own thought—rather than "framing" it with quotation marks that separate it off (criticism comes from Gk. *krinein*, to separate!)

                    & going over the transcript i see the way we talk is a kind of matrix, often collaborative as we repeat each other's phrasing, carrying someone else's words into our own comments, or adding our own words to another's unfinished sentence

—there we were, curled or slouched in separate chairs with our individual coffees, our individual positions in the conversation—ideas twining together in the space between us, or brought up short with an asserted difference, but then finding another way to grow, elaborate from the difference itself

                    ~ ~ ~

Vancouver. Aug. 12. 83

looking again at Gail's W[omen &] W[ords] paper ["Shaping a Vehicle for Her Use"], there's something i deeply recognize in what she says about "the difficulty of asserting one's own *way of seeing*": "the temptation is often to concentrate on making 'sense' of what we are experiencing, to explain, to justify. And this gets us caught up in patriarchal concepts of time, space, causality" which "sometimes prevent us from exploring a deeper reality."

                    —Yes! this "difficulty" is what my novel is composed of,

her attempt (Annie's) to find a way of speaking her reality without going mad, as her mother does, or fading into silence as Ana Richards does

Gail speaks of "the fractured female identity, the difficulty of centring self, of knowing self" as actually <u>situated</u> in the gap between 2 languages: our "undernourished woman's voice, not heard outside in what our mothers always said was a 'man's world'" (so her mother said that too! a woman's phrase generations old?) & the language of fatherland, the patriarchy as it is embedded in the justice system, educational texts, media—the language of reason, of consequences ("of consequence" because it deals with "consequences," punishment & rewards, inclusions & exclusions)

mothertongue on the other hand speaks out of psychic interrelatedness, simultaneity, the multifoliate (rose)—at best, the poem

so many points of connection—all these essays coming in for *Tessera*, for the Women & Words proceedings—so much that is vital to our sense of direction—that pushes me to think, articulate, more clearly & "in concert"—to be reading & corresponding with such vibrant & creative women is like having an ear to a party phone-line, only the level of exchange is much more crucial, has so much more at stake

~ ~ ~

Vancouver. Sept. 27. 83.

Linda Rogers' poems to Maggie Jack in *Queens of the Next Hot Star*, including prose poems written in the voices of Maggie's friends or neighbours, including objects, myths, dreams, private history Maggie has told her over the years—

& Bronwen Wallace's "Cancer Poems" in *Signs of the Former Tenant*, the dream poems, dreams she had herself or dreams her dying friend told her?, the poems about the doctor, exploratory surgery, treatment must have been built of details her friend told her—

—i'm moved by the commonality of women's lives, the sharing here, & the love so evident—Linda & Bronwen pass on the experiences of Maggie & the unnamed friend for us to share—not so much taking something private but enlarging something we all inherit: our lives, deaths & how we sense our being in them—

i can't see this sharing as a betrayal of confidence or privacy—i think of Sheila's fear of betraying another's privacy which proposes a view of writing as an invasion, as predatory—notions of privacy are only glass walls set up to prevent us experiencing our commonality, our undefined common wealth, which more & more i'm getting a sense of—just as i begin to understand that privacy/property, which are the same (propriété) in French, the properness of it all, the legitimizing, the ethic of owning through the male line—this obsession with privacy/property masks the fear that what is owned may be taken away—we are coming to see that what we experience in common as women is what we share underneath the glass fences & private front doors—life is too terrifyingly closed & isolated otherwise

~ ~ ~

Fragment from a letter to Gail Scott strategizing over the articulation of the Tessera *theme* Reading and Writing, *for a guest issue which Gail proposed to* La nouvelle barre du jour *(Montreal). In September 1995 the issue appeared as NBJ 157, our collective's second issue.*

Vancouver. Dec 21. 83

Dear Gail*:

my apologies for taking longer to reply than i wanted or intended to. But here, to answer your questions:

* Gail Scott

Orientation: you might use Hélène Cixous—i'm quoting from the Eng.
translation of "The Laugh of the Medusa" in *New French Feminisms*:
speaking of "this emancipation of the marvellous text of her self that she
must urgently learn to speak"—that the feminist orientation on writing
as reading would involve writing as a reading of this "text of her self"
which is so far unspoken & the very act of writing is at one & the same
time a reading (in the sense that you read your present as others read
the future, as a palmist reads a palm, say) of a text that is not spelled
out because it is the text(ure) of a life that you're inside of, reading by
touch. & that much of new feminist writing involves an active reading of
the language <u>as it arises</u> in your mouth or on the page—in two ways:
1) to read "beyond" or "through" the patriarchal loading of the language &
2) to read out from your own vocabulary of resonant terms what it is
that is particularly yours, your bodily experience, your history, your myth,
buried there &, once read out/elucidated, led into the light [for others to
read]. then reading as translation. variant readings on a text. that that
is the other interest in reading as writing, the composing anew of already
written texts, the building on each other's work, the weaving-in to a new
matrix that is also the ongoing continually developing collective text—in
fact i've asked the women i've asked to contribute to the issue to think
not only of how writing is reading in their own work but how their reading
of other women's texts becomes (their) writing.

~ ~ ~

Vancouver. Aug. 8. 84

stories occur in time: that is the nature of their narrative build-up—

how have a character who doesn't develop? what is the interest then? or
is it that women are so interested in development (narrative/emotional)
as an analogue for self-liberation?

the old motif: i remember Diane & i walking up the road from school,
balancing our books on our heads to develop "better posture," criticizing

each other for how we slouched or spoke, or for the clothes we wore—for failing, in short, to live up to those 1950s images of femininity we carried in our heads—which we never thought of as "images," only as the real, as who we were meant to become

as Louky's Aphélie says in *Le Pique-nique:* "L'histoire de l'humanité qu'on nous a donnée pour *vraie* est un grand roman de science-fiction plein de monstres fabuleux et de beautés extra-terrestres [i.e., women made extra-terrestrial because they are put on the margins of space & time, made unreal, anachronic in their idealized beauty]; un grand roman policier aussi, plein *de meurtres anonymes où l'on a fait disparaître les corps,* où l'on a parfaitement fait disparaître les taches de sang, de sorte que les gens ne croient pas à la réalité de ces meurtres."

~ ~ ~

Vancouver. Aug. 10. 84

labyrinth (Webster's): a structure full of intricate passageways that make it difficult to find the way from the interior to the entrance or from the entrance [en-trance-d still by the exterior] to the interior [one's centre?]

the labyrinth on Crete constructed by Daedalus to confine the Minotaur [to update, what if we imagine the Minotaur as a woman, one of Louky's *monstres?*]

.... a maze [a-maze-d by her place in a male-dominated culture]

.... a complex that baffles exploration—"the labyrinth of a great novel" E.K. Brown—[the socio-cultural novel we are en-trance-d in: what we are conditioned to see as the real—a complex that baffles exit]

a situation or state of mind from which it is difficult to extricate oneself

West Word

Summer School/Retreat for Women

August 4-18, 1985
at the Vancouver School of Theology—UBC

Brought to you by
West Coast Women & Words Society of British Columbia

Summer School Course

I Poetry

The instructor will provide assistance in criticising and polishing individual poems, as well as examining modern poetics and recent trends in Canadian poetry. There will be group workshops, readings, and individual consultations.

II Fiction

Workshop/instruction will assist writers in improving style, structure, and narrative techniques.

There will be opportunity for reading and reworking within class time.

III Playwriting

This course is aimed at writers wishing to hone their skills in creating dramatic material for stage, television, or radio. Participants will consider dramatic styles, dialogue-writing, contemporary stagecraft and the technical requirements of each medium. Opportunity for "cold" readings will be provided.

Studies

Instructor: **Daphne Marlatt** (Vancouver)

Daphne's thirteen books include *Steveston*, *How Hug a Stone*, and, most recently, *Touch to My Tongue*. She has taught writing workshops throughout Canada and will soon take the position of writer in residence at the University of Alberta.

Guest Speaker: **Dorothy Livesay** (Galiano Island)

One of Canada's most esteemed writers, Dorothy has published books of poetry for more than 50 years. Her latest is *Feeling the World*. She was a founding member of the League of Canadian Poets and the founding editor of CV/II, a quarterly of Canadian poetry and criticism.

Instructor: **Gail Scott** (Montreal)

Gail worked as a journalist before turning to fiction writing full-time. She co-founded the Montreal French-language literary review, *Spirale*. Recently she lectured at the Kootenay School of Writing on new feminist writing. Coach House published *Spare Parts*, a collection of short stories, in 1983.

Guest Speaker: **Jane Rule** (Galiano Island)

Jane writes novels, short stories, and essays. Most recently published are *Hot-Eyed Moderate* and *Inland Passage*. Her stories and essays have appeared in numerous magazines and anthologies.

Instructor: **Margaret Hollingsworth** (Toronto)

Playwright, fiction writer, and teacher of writing; Margaret was recently writer in residence at Concordia University. Her plays, which include *Islands*, *Everloving*, and *War Baby* have been produced in theatres, on radio, and television.

Guest Speaker: **Patricia Ludwick** (Vancouver)

A professional theatre artist Patricia's plays include *Alone*, and *Letter to My Goddaughter*. *Trip the Light Fantastic* was produced at Vancouver's New Play Centre. She has taught theatre arts at Langara and the New Play Centre.

Writing Our Way Through the Labyrinth

This brief musing on the cultural significance of reading as both distinct from and as part of writing was written for NBJ 157, "l'Écriture comme lecture," our Tessera guest-issue which appeared in September 1985. I saw it as a way of cross-pollinating my own idiosyncratic odyssey through reading and writing with larger cultural meanings associated with those activities.

Writing and Reading. two of the three R's every child learns in school (forgetting, for the moment, that one of the two begins with *w*). to commonalize them, writing and reading go together like speaking and hearing, ancient uses of the eye, the ear, the hand, each informing the other. i was taught to write by sound, taught to form the letters of words that together formed lines of memorized poetry, deciphering as i went what the letters were saying, then following the curve of syntax, its twists and turns, as i made the curving up-and-down of letters forming Walter de la Mare's words: *Slowly, silently, now the moon / Walks the night in her silver shoon. . . .*

and so caught from then on, intrigued by the twists and turns of the labyrinth of language. an ancient structure i found my way into (or my teachers led me to, leaving me alone with the thread in my hands), full of interconnecting passageways, trapdoors, melodious charms, vivid and often incomprehensible images on the walls, all of them pointing, pointing me farther along—the thread, the desire to know, *gno*—, narrative, tugging in my hands. lifeline (trying to make sense of it all). the pull of syntax (arranged in order) i felt my way by. trying to find something familiar, something i recognized:

so i could be found in the midst of all these meanings pointing elsewhere.

later as i began to write (compose) poetry, i learned that writing involves reading or hearing all the language is saying that i am "lost" in and writing my way through. as if following the thread of meaning through the labyrinth of language (through its walls echoing with other texts) requires an inner ear, a sensory organ i feel my way by (sentence, *sentire,* to feel), keeping my feet by a labyrinthine sense of balance as the currents of various meanings, the unexpected "drift," swirl me along. of course the labyrinth is filled with fluid, as the membranous labyrinth of the inner ear is. women know the slippery feel of language, the walls that exclude us, the secret passageways of double meaning that conduct us into a sense we understand, reverberant with hidden meaning, the meaning our negated (in language) bodies radiate. bodies that possess no singular authoritative meaning but meaning that is manifold, multilabial and continuously arrived at.

labyrinth: a structure consisting of a number of intercommunicating passages arranged in a bewildering complexity. labyrinth: "not a maze to get lost in; it had only one path, traversing all parts of the figure" (Walker 523). labyrinth: a continuous walking that folds back on itself and in folding back moves forward. labyrinth: earth-womb, underground, a journeying to the underworld and back. House of the Double Axe, sceptre of the Cretan Moon-Goddess (here she is again, in her silver shoon). intercommunicating passages circling back.

but those are some of the images on the walls. and if we examine the bricks? the basics? (re-reading with a feminist ear for re-verb-(h)er-ation?) writing goes back to a Germanic word, *writan,* meaning to tear, scratch, cut, incise. the act of the phallic singular, making its mark on things (stone, wood, sand, paper). leaving its track, "I was here," the original one in the world. reading, however, goes back to Indo-European *ar-*, to fit together, which appears in Old English as *raedan,* to advise, explain, read. the relational seems foremost: advising and caring for are aspects which still survive in the word *rede,* counsel or advice given, a decision taken by one or more persons. even in the usual sense of reading, "to look over or scan (something written, printed, etc.) with understanding of what is meant by the letters or signs," there is this relating what the writer meant to what the reader understands, a commune-ication the word writing seems not to carry from its root.

this deep desire to "stand in for" (the other), to understand something other than what one knows oneself, comes to the fore in phrases such as reading the future, reading one's palm. "The sense of considering or explaining something obscure or mysterious is also common to the various languages, but the application of this to the interpretation of ordinary writing, and to the expression of this in speech, is confined to Eng. and ON (Old Norse) (in the latter perhaps under Eng. influence)," says the OED. reading what we are in the mi(d)st of. reading the world. reading one's body, that vast text (sixty thousand miles of veins and arteries). writing, the act of the singular, and reading, the act of the plural, of the more than one, of the one in relation to others.

in a time when language has been appropriated by the neo-Freudians as intrinsically phallic—as Xavière Gauthier explains it, "the linear, grammatical, linguistic system that orders the symbolic, the superego, the law . . . is a system based entirely on one fundamental signifier: the phallus" (162)—it seems crucial to reclaim language through what we know of ourselves in relation to writing. writing can scarcely be for women the act of the phallic signifier, its claim to singularity, the mark of the capital I (was here). language is no "tool" for us, no extension of ourselves, but something we are "lost" inside of (Warland 1987). finding our way in a labyrinthine moving with the drift, slipping through claims to one-track meaning so that we can recover multiply-related meanings, reading between the lines. finding in write, rite, growing out of *ar-*, that fitting together at the root of reading (we circle back), moving into related words for arm, shoulder (joint), harmony—the music of connection. making our way through all parts of the figure, using our labyrinthine sense, we (w)rite our way *ar-* way, reading and relating these intercommunicating passages.

Vancouver. November 1. 84.

reading Smaro's ms. last night [Kamboureli, *in the second person*], the agonizing split of the self between Greek/Canadian, the being out of touch with who one was, that old self defined by the old place, yet never accepted in the new place as of it—i realize Annie has to write more about Ina's immigrant isolation, how it enables her to see clearly what she isn't a part of

—Smaro's sense of the lost self or ghost self tied to a language that is not the language of her intellect—limbo: between definitions of self—or lost in the labyrinth

the desired self the lost one in her logbook of the Orphic journey: "to look back would mean . . . to marry the possibility of a re-encounter with my past . . . to be caressed by memories that belong to my other." caressed: she captures so well the sensual pull of those memories that rise up suddenly from a past place/self, another rhythm, smell, touch super-imposed on this here—so outside language yet the word points to it

the desired self is a future one too: "[immigration] is a desire for a yet unknown object, a desire that kills its 'subject.'"—that paradox time plays out in coming to be Canadian: that it involves a sort of amputation, a gradual loss of parts

~ ~ ~

Vancouver. Nov. 9 84

that first (or second?) prose poem (in a Sixties California poetry mag i somehow associate with Ed Dorn), where i located myself in the ditch on the far side of town lurking there with the other witches (Di Prima was one): a sort of pre-dyke poem, bristling with the sense of being other—years before i read Brossard or Wittig's narrative mosaic, *Les Guerillères* —or Bersianik's subverted Platonic (ma-tonic) dialogues in *le Pique-nique*—or Daly's radical de- & re-codings of "The Word" now, twenty years after that early poem the writing witches are building, have built, their own piazza in the centre of town—this sense of shared ground coming into view, into articulate presence—& yet, as a writer, where am i? somewhere in the gap between the social realism of most Anglo women's writing & the "fiction-theory" of Québécoise feminists— drawn to the "strange familiarity" of abstraction, yet attached to the specific details of a life & still in love with the sensory image—which <u>can</u> leap, can luxuriate beyond realist convention—god knows, we NEED the analysis, yet there's also that strong pull to narrative, even the loosest kind, & a lyrically charged language coincident with it

~ ~ ~

Vancouver. Nov. 11. 84

Bonnie Zimmerman's article on lesbian personal narratives:

talks about politics at that intersection of truth & coverup which has to be constantly negotiated in the risky "fact" of being lesbian—she counters the move towards theory in heterosexual feminist writing with what she calls a tendency in lesbian writing to stick with personal narrative (what about Wittig? Brossard?—they're not American) & accounts for the difference between the 2 trends with the continually necessary process of coming out:

"Speaking, especially naming one's self 'lesbian,' is an act of empowerment. Power, which traditionally is the essence of politics, is connected with the ability to name, to speak, to come out of silence. . . . Powerlessness, on the other hand, is associated with silence and the 'speechlessness' that the powerful impose on those dispossessed of language. In a sense, then, contemporary lesbian feminists postulate lesbian oppression as a mutilation of consciousness curable by language." —powerful image, "mutilation"—& what she says about the power of self-naming is true—but why does the language-cure have to be limited to self-affirmation?

she herself is wary of "a politics based so strongly on personal identity"
& adds: "Perhaps we need to refocus our attention on the connecting
exchange of language, rather than on the isolating structure of identity,
allowing our political language to derive richness & variety from its many
dialects, idioms, & even ungrammatical idiosyncracies."

that phrase, "the connecting exchange of language"—yes, where
identities themselves can shift—the Demeter-Kore exchange [in *Touch
to my Tongue*]

~ ~ ~

Edmonton. Oct. 11. 85

trying to negotiate the streets here is like trying to escape the gap
between the map we carry in our heads and concrete reality—it gives rise
to passionate arguments. Betsy drives while i try to "navigate" but the
map, so gridlike and clear on paper with its numbered streets & avenues,
its compass quadrants SW, NE, etc., turns out to contain unexpected
dead ends, a block taken up by some industrial yard or building. if i
remember the street number, but not whether it's really a street
(instead of an avenue), we end up miles away on the wrong side of town.
who conceived this city? who started numbering from preconceived limits
towards the centre? somebody who thought the map was final, thought
it could determine growth, impose order. i miss Vancouver's oddly named
& curving streets, i miss the sea & its inroads, their incessant rising
& draining, evidence of what we can contain perhaps but not control

~ ~ ~

excerpt from notes for a talk in the spring of 1986 to a University of Alberta class on lesbian literature:

rethinking the muse for a lesbian writer (or, what inspires you?):

Rachel Blau Duplessis says that for H.D. lesbianism was not a "sufficient strategy of solution to the cultural problem posed by males" (21) because, subject as she was to bouts of "thralldom" to inspirational male writers/figures in her life (Pound, Aldington, Lawrence, Freud), she needed validation from her male peers

but what H.D. lacked in her own time & what we now have is a strong feminist audience whose validation can be as powerful as male validation was for her—the experience of a <u>community</u> of female readers who are women-centred & lesbian-affiliated

in "Tender Skin My Mind" Nicole Brossard beautifully articulates the importance of a sense of identifying with/belonging to a specifically lesbian community:

"Being colonized means not thinking for oneself, but thinking through others, putting one's emotions at the service of others, in short not existing [the voiceless muse!] and above all being unable to find in the group one belongs to the sources of inspiration and motivation essential to any artistic production. It is essential to find in the group one belongs to captivating images which can nourish us spiritually, intellectually and emotionally" (180–81)

she says that women motivate her "to change life, language, and society" (181) & that lesbians inspire her because "we are a challenge for the imaginary, and in a certain sense for ourselves, insofar as we bring ourselves into the world" (181). since patriarchal consciousness (in men or women) conceives of women only in reference to men, lesbian love is something such consciousness can barely imagine she talks about "being at the origin of sense": making our own sense, first with our bodies (which are literally in the world & which we must take as the literal basis for our writing) & secondly with our energy & skill which fire our desire—for it is desire "which sets us in movement toward sense" (181)

—here we have a radical redefinition of making sense which insists on the primacy of "rethinking the world"— & of course then of rethinking language since it is with language that we compose & communicate our world

rethinking pronouns as a lesbian writer:

in her introduction to *Lesbian Body*, Monique Wittig points to a crisis the woman writer has with even so basic a unit of language as the personal pronoun *je*, which she says she cannot use because it contains no gender marking & therefore pretends to be universal, which we know usually means male—so she splits it, *j/e*, to dramatize not only this split in the speaking subject who is female, but her exclusion as a lesbian—a double split, which "throughout literature is the exercise of a language which does not constitute m/e as subject" (10–11)

the question Wittig raises: can lesbian writers convey the full range of our experience by writing only from the position of the periphery, being on the fringe of the heterosexual, let alone patriarchal world, still being in reference to it? what if we assume ourselves at centre, as Brossard does in her writing? & further, what if we assume ourselves already whole?

this would involve a writing that examines the shifting relations between i + you (both un-gender-marked) + she + she, let alone he—as well as the fixed & oppositional us + them: to undo that opposition, place the lesbian i at centre of her world & finger the variegated strands of the network of relations she is in the midst of & which she reorders by her very presence —a reworking that parallels Duplessis' call for "the reordering of family, sexes, psyche" that functions as muse for the woman writer—a reordering that is radical with two women-lovers as the heart of a new family that can embrace one or the other's children, blood-relatives, friends & their children, all considered family—psyche has been so often mapped in terms of the nuclear oedipal family: this revised family would call for revised approaches not only to social gender role but to psyche itself

~ ~ ~

Lesbera

This essay fuses two earlier pieces. The first was written as a series of comments to preface a reading at the University of Alberta where i spent the winter of 1985–1986 as writer-in-residence. The second, under the above title, was written for our "Changing the Subject" issue of Tessera *(no. 9, fall 1990).*

Lesbera—to coin a portmanteau word (yes, an old-fashioned carry-all with two compartments) for two sets of musings about lesbian identity. A term derived not from Catullus' actively sexual but straight hetaera, Lesbia, but from a sense of what the possibilities are now for poetic lesbian erotica. A term to map a position at the crossroads of lesbian + era, within the rather brief tradition of lesbian representation and in relation to the raw (nonverbal) power of erotic desire. Poem and map, desiring rush and lineage.

So, first: era.

To look for a lesbian tradition beyond the Modernist period is to realize that, except for Sappho of Lesbos, whose seventh century B.C. love poems to young women gave early twentieth-century writers like Natalie Barney the word itself, our tradition is largely unwritten, and when it has been written, it may be written in code, like Gertrude Stein's love poems to Alice Toklas. If the history of women has been largely overlooked in the records, trivialized as unimportant, set aside as mundane and oh-so-cyclical, certainly not climactic—(and we're not talking about the erotic here—or maybe we are, maybe the linear

shape of history has been determined by a phallic sense of the erotic?)—if women's history has been overlooked, then lesbian history has
definitely been swept under the carpet, into the closet. Kept out of
sight as something immoral, mutant, shameful—not, by any means, a
tradition we might glory in.

Radclyffe Hall was the first to publicly address, even batter at, that
closet door. Her now-classic novel, *The Well of Loneliness*, presents
Stephen as a congenital "invert" who has no other moral choice than
to accept her nature and live it out as honourably (on conventionally
male terms of honour) as she can. Hall's novel accurately depicts her
period's prevailing attitude towards dykes, lesbians, cross-dressers and
gays, but it accedes to the depressing weight of that view of gender
deviance as pathological. Virginia Woolf, on the other hand, was the
first to transform the closet into a shifting and multilevelled theatre of
gender. In the novel named after her central character, she has
Orlando physically transform from male to female as casually as s/he
changes costume and lovers through historical periods and foreign
lands, all with great verve and verbal wit. Not marginalized at all,
Orlando occupies the centre of his world and transports the reader
into the world of his gender-"other," rendered equally present and
central as Orlando/she. Here, language play reflects Woolf's play with
gender definitions.

These two approaches, which i might characterize as a lesbian realist
resistance to marginalization (with accompanying analysis of oppression) and an inspired revelling in gender alternatives, have
characterized a tradition as varied as Audre Lorde's *Zami* and Nicole
Brossard's *French Kiss*. Both approaches are necessary and perhaps
extensions of each other. For it seems to me that in refusing the con-

dition of marginalization, we are coming to an expanded notion of what (and who) "women" might embrace, leaving behind those concepts Hall had to struggle with, lesbians as half-women, mutants lurking on the edges of womanhood. If we take the narrow Victorian concept of womanhood (still unfortunately current in the expectation that women do the emotional work in heterosexual relationships), if we re-vise it to include the widest human potential for loving, then the loving of other women can be a source of knowledge about our own being, our full erotic, spiritual and historic potential. This is neither meant to blur lesbian difference nor minimize the actual hazards of living out dyke lives in a homophobic society. It seems to me that refusing an obsession with our marginalization, refusing the limits of that self-definition, is the first step towards realizing a larger understanding of who we are.

We live both inside history and inside imagination. As Nicole Brossard has pointed out, so often and so beautifully, we have to invent ourselves because a lesbian, the fully lived life of a lesbian, cannot be imagined within the confines of patriarchal thought. Women enter history, for instance, as the daughters or wives or mothers of powerful men, as perhaps "the power behind the throne," women who bent the system but used their influence to secure the status of their families within it. Straight history, the stuff of historical romance.

Yet, if we look, we find the "crazy women," women who tried to make changes on their own without the aid of fathers or husbands, women who got wiped out because they were regarded as possessed or evil, like Joan of Arc, like thousands of nameless witches. Women who ran head-on into the stone walls of western patriarchal thought, which is blind to wisdom or moral or spiritual strength in alternative forms of thought. The vaunting of conquest, of imperial domination, of male right to power by the strongest male with the greatest technological advantage, is a cruel hoax on human potential. This vaunting is the stuff of western history, which traces the gradual wiping out of other forms of socialization, of consciousness, of reality on this planet.

But the crazy women are the keys to our alternative "herstory," which involves the rewriting of history. As Cixous puts it, "What woman hasn't flown/stolen? Who hasn't felt, dreamt, performed the gesture that jams sociality? who hasn't crumbled, held up to ridicule, the bar of separation?" (258). The crazy women live inside our heads, nourished by our crazy mothers, our rebel contemporaries, our self-selected heroines, the wild "failures" we love. And also fear.

This fear gets in the way of our imagination. I want to bring it as close to home as the question "Who is your mother?" As Paula Gunn Allen remarks in an essay which bears this question as its title, "Failure to know your mother. . . . is the same as being lost" (209). Now we white lesbians don't identify ourselves by clan; often we can't even identify ourselves within our nuclear families. But the Native concept of mother doesn't just involve a biological mother; it involves, as Gunn Allen says, "an entire generation of women whose psychic, and consequently physical, 'shape' made the psychic existence of the following generation possible" (209). The desperation of the struggle for physical survival is not something all of us have experienced. But the struggle for psychic survival is, and often and not least at the hands of our mothers who cannot accept our deviancy from the narrow path they trod. Gunn Allen's larger definition offers an alternative and much more affirmative understanding of mothering. For our own survival we need to know not only our biological mothers but our historical foremothers and our literary mothers, those whose work helps us begin to recognize the largeness of who we are or can be.

Getting to know our various mothers involves "seeing through" or past the smallness of how they have been viewed by patriarchal eyes. It involves embracing the so-called minor, the so-called failed, the so-called damaged and deviant, in them as well as ourselves—so that we can see the power in these psychic spaces, these gaps in the patriarchal system we occupy. Our mothers precede and surround us with the evidence of their visions, however lived out. It is up to us to see them.

~ ~ ~

And that other compartment/component of *lesbera*: the erotic.

To speak or write rationally of the erotic, to discuss it at all, is only to touch its shadow. Because the erotic as i actually experience it, as i imagine any of you do, is raw power, a current surging through my body surging beyond the limits of self-containment, beyond the limits of syntax and logic and of the daily order that keeps me organizing time into small manageable chunks tailored to the work at hand.

Erotic energy in free play doesn't have much to do with a careful, even parsimonious, parcelling out. It doesn't have much to do with measure or even measuring up, to any standard set by some conventional authority.

The erotic has everything to do with immediacy and presence, though it is not self-contained. Like water or fire, it seeks to go beyond limits, above all beyond the limits of self as distinct from other. This surging through my arteries and meridians spills toward yours, a surging between us we feel electrical—the "turn-on"—we feel magnetic, flashy as lightning, magnetized and lost, and at the same time enlarged, more than life-size in its presence. We feel in flight and risky with relief from the temporal, we could hazard aerial acrobatics grounded deep in each other's groins, we will birth ourselves apparitional and strange, the mouth that groans a shout, the vulva that pushes out to touch/be touched, legs that gape wide for the subterranean rush of coming. In that rush we may *sound* the erotic, but we can't speak of it. And when we write it later, we write an after-image, an altered imprint of that bodily burning.

And yet, when we write, there is something in the erotics of language that sets up another kind of surging. Different yet similar, it surges beyond the limits of orderly syntax and established meaning. When we get right down to it, the erotic is anti-authority, always has been.

If you look up the figure of Eros, who gives us the word, you find capriciousness, mischief, anarchy on the wing. The trouble with the classical tradition as we have inherited it in English (and in French, for that matter) is that the erotic is heterosexually based. It is the realm of a troublemaking male sprite we remember in Valentine images of Cupid with his bow and oh-so-phallic arrow. Arrow and the object of desire. The object's pain at the unlooked-for arrow, the mist of deception, being at the mercy of the comings and goings of Eros: all these associations derive from the patriarchal Greeks. Where does that leave women's desire and especially women's desire for women? What images do we have for a woman-based erotic?

The lesbian subject: the woman-mouth that pushes out to assert its touch, its reach for the other's hidden mouth shouting through all its aroused lips "lesbian." The mutual recognition, anarchic and wild— and then these images we have that run against the social grain of straight culture: the Amazon, bull-dyke, witch, virago. Women who have too much—power, strength, knowledge, sense of ourselves, of our own desire.

Paula Gunn Allen writes of a very different tradition, the Native one where, amongst the Lakota, the *koskalaka,* the woman who is seen as a "young man" who doesn't want to marry, at least not marry a man, is regarded in a spiritual context as having medicine power (257). This is a power that Nicole Brossard translates into a physicalized and erotic writing as "the feel of tongues, the patience/ of mouths devoting themselves to understanding/ integral" (1986 32). Judy Grahn retrieves from obscurity a poetic lineage for this power which she names "[t]he Lesbian *civitas*" or "community . . . located here in the world of cold and hot factuality . . . here with its mysticism and its forces intact" (131). Getting in touch with our desire as lesbians can be a source of power, as Audrey Lorde has pointed out. The lesbian erotic as power, not something split off, denigrated, mutant. In this sense the power of the erotic is something we come into as we gain our full identity as women unconfined by the crippling dualisms of western culture.

We are a changed subject. Our erotic has to do with the power of reversal and contradiction speaking against the so-called "norms," the so-called reality, small and constraining, we were told to fit inside of. Breaking free, we have undergone a not so subtle change in the way we recognize other women and ourselves as sources of that electric, magnetic power of awakened connection flaring across the rifts that separate us in the colonial and classist world we inhabit. As changed subjects we are no longer preoccupied with patriarchal power. We occupy ourselves with recognizing and activating the power to connect we feel as fully charged subjects in our own erotic light. Powerhouses, transformers, live wires, we touch each other into mutual being.

To mark eros with lesbian identity: a new word, *lesbera,* the *lesberetic* (yes, heretic) expression of erotic power as a transforming energy we revel in each time we move our lovers, our readers and ourselves to that ecstatic surging beyond limits. Each time we follow the language-surge of connection writing beyond conventional limits across the page.

*backtracking now to Vancouver and 1985 again, in order to trace
through another and simultaneous concern. the linear form of a book
requires separating out (the better to follow) what are interconnecting threads
in a longstanding labyrinth of preoccupations.*

Vancouver. Feb. 20. 85.

the trouble with plot in *Ana H.*—not wanting a plot-driven novel but not
knowing what shape a looser sense of narrative might take—don't want
a sense of moral order to dominate the characters. perhaps because i'd
rather write something akin to a long poem—something with a more
inclusive sense of knowing/narrating—want to know all the relations that
can exist between 2 words, 2 images, 2 characters, & more.

as Adrienne Rich says in *Lies, Secrets & Silence,* "Poetry is above all a
concentration of the *power* of language, which is the power of our ultimate
relationship to everything in the universe."

so the narrative, the knowing, is that sense
of knowing how & to whom, to what we are both ultimately & immediately
related. for a woman poet, it involves "everywhere she has been" (Rich)—
re-reading every space, every state, every relationship she has come
through to be at this point, this intersection of word & paper. not lopping
anything off. for our own survival, both personal & species-oriented, we
need a sense of narrative as inclusive as this—a narrative that registers
the importance of the smallest intricate relations we live among & which,
from an ecological & feminist understanding, <u>support</u> us & our single-
minded preoccupations.

~ ~ ~

Vancouver. July ? 85.

putting together some news from the theoretical edge of Can. lit. crit.
(which does bring news, though i balk at it):

Pat Smart's article in *Canadian Forum* on Québécois & English-Canadian
cultures, her focus on the realism of Eng-Can lit: "In the work of poets like
Roberts, Lampman, F.R. Scott, Dorothy Livesay, Earle Birney and Al
Purdy language is, taken for granted and used as a means of entry into
reality, while for Emile Nelligan, Saint-Denys Garneau, and even for a
political poet like Gaston Miron, a primary focus is not reality but the
voyage within language itself" which, she says, explodes the "prison" of
landscape through its play—

what she says about the realism-landscape-language link
is useful but her focus is so mainstream—it's true she gives a nod in the
direction of postmodern writing but mentions only one woman when there
are so many she <u>could</u> have mentioned who are already exploding
the confines of realism—why not talk about their work? can't help
wondering: if our tradition is defined as realist, then is a non-transparent,
not-merely-realist use of language somehow un-Canadian? what about
Sheila Watson? Phyllis Webb?

then there's Barbara's essay in the current *Can. Forum* (basically her
Women & Words paper) which also contrasts Anglo-Can. women writers
& Québécoise ones, looking at how much less radical & more "complacent"
Anglo writers are—her comments on the 2 different traditions of
feminist language-theory compact a lot of reading into a few interesting
observations:

—she too talks about realism & the Anglo "suspicion of
language" (her model seems to be Atwood, also mainstream), which leads
to a "retreat from the logos and the word into sensation, finding refuge in
realistic forms of communication," in "writing as transcription, translation
of sensation"—whereas Quebec women writers "inscribe themselves in
the body of language" & consequently "avoid the concept of translation

and its valorizing of a single centre," a single reality—her model here is Brossard, who she says "substitutes for [translation of sensation] an emphasis on reading (and unreading)"

—Barbara seems to be reading Eng-Can. fiction, not poetry—or at least not some poetry where that transformative aspect of language constantly shifts how we see the solid walls of image thought passes through—

so here i am, identifying as a poet, with a strong pull towards narrative— how relate the two?—narrative that doesn't follow a clue to some single centre so much as follow the twists & turns of language, where it gets me to in this labyrinth without a centre—language not utilitarian, something to "get me there"—where after all? there's nowhere but here: its radiance of meanings "duplicit" (as Cotnoir says) or multiplicit, many-levelled

~ ~ ~

Narrative in Language Circuits

During my year as writer-in-residence at the University of Alberta, bp Nichol came to read and we both spoke on narrative as we saw it operating in the long poem, particularly as we found it working in our own compositional processes. These talks were subsequently published in The Dinosaur Review 8 *(summer 1986). This seems the third in a set of "musings."*

a narrative, a story, a description of events, is made of language, yes, but in the composition of a poem, any poem, not necessarily a narrative poem, are we being drawn into a narrative that is *in* language? that is the "telling" power of language?

language is larger than us and carries us along with it. matrix image. matrix on the move. rapid current. (rapid as the neural one.) born(e) along the onward movement of association, we ride a building wave of meaning, cresting incrementally—but wait, the water breaks, spray flies. narrative *in* language seems to be less a line, falling into place as neatly as the body of the wave does—less a line than a web. which we spin, sound, volley along. by which we are held, told, spun into larger and larger reaches of meaning.

this is not a matter of the narrative line which the reader pursues (a line of crumbs, say, clues) into the thick of the telling and out again. "Getting from the beginning to the end of a statement is simple movement," Lyn Hejinian writes, whereas "following the connotative by-ways . . . is complex or compound movement" (139). compound interest which accumulates along the way. a complex of connections, compelling, yes, whose patterns are less habitual than revealed. "Language discovers what one might know, which in turn is always less than what language might say" (Hejinian 138).

generative, language as matrix surrounds us (hands up! fingering those synaptic points where word transmits word, phrase, a whole idea rooted in a syllable, phoneme), a tissue of poetic words, say, each of them "polyvalent and multi-determined" (Kristeva 65). these words constantly touch on each other, touch each other in sound(ing) reaches of meaning beyond the narrative line as such. if the narrative line is plumb, then what it plumbs stretches beyond it in every direction. the horizon line of language extends always beyond each individual speaker/writer, no matter how you turn.

perhaps here we come up against a phrase bp Nichol has used, "the secret narrative . . . of your compositional process" (308), which, he says, the postmodernist writer can't get away from. perhaps this leaves us with overt narrative as the narrative line, what is being recounted in sequence from beginning to end. or what the poem is "about"—though that word is "about" so much: in reference to (a particular, say) as well as on all sides, surrounding. it used to mean on the outside of, which is probably what we mean when we try to answer the question, "What is bp Nichol's *The Martyrology* or my *Steveston* about?" as if the "about" were the exoskeleton of the work, ossified. what we are left with.

on the inside then (the vital process of the inside) is the secret narrative of your neural engagement with the web, the network. intersecting lines of communication. touch-points that fire multi-byways of meaning. in the "continuous present" of composing, to use

Stein's phrase, you are definitely inside language. being fired by it. critically "in touch."

touch words. touch points, touch wood. used to fire other wood. would (that which covers distance, "if wishes were horses . . ."). narrative must be the distance covered in writing.

each of us has particular touch words. words we spend a lifetime of writing unravelling through to their ends (which are not ends but means to larger and larger implications, foldings-in). composing or putting them together means being in touch at least two ways: with the particulars of your own experience touched off by certain words and with the more that language might say—kindling, in their interplay, what the poem can and does say.

a long poem offers the scope for such word/thought unravellings: most clearly, the "chains" evolving in Book V of *The Martyrology* that spin the writer/reader into alternate byways. the unravelling of "language" for instance in the bilingual/alphabetic pun: "l'an g / which is the year seven," which takes us into word transformations losing *g,* or else "l'an g / u age" which moves into a counting of the visionary years. in *How Hug a Stone* (which my publisher advertised as a novel but which i wrote as a cycle of prose poems) word chains occur subtextually. one that runs through several poems—"guest, obliged, hostly & hostile, ghostly"—branches into "tomb, womb, earth" in touch with "guest" again (the body "hosted" by earth in Neolithic grave ceremonies). these are touch points, touch words in the "secret narrative" of the compositional process. connecting points of the neural net language makes of experience, where light flares. moving along the net we find it moves through us and the distance covered is circuit-us. in all ways.

Penny's Cottages, Galiano Island Dec. 2. 87

reading Mary's [Meigs] *The Box Closet*—her analysis of engagement & marriage is brilliant—makes me think about the fulcrum of sex, of coming into sexual activity

for the novel: 2 parallels, or maybe not, maybe 2 distinct lines which merge & cross at some point:
the coming to sexuality of my mother in marriage (the taboos of the period—my grandmother's making sure "the goods" were virginal in body & mind by refusing to even speak of sex to her—if she had no knowledge of what to expect then that would prove her "unspoiled")

the coming to lesbian self-knowledge of her daughter so many years later—the slowness of the process, the taboos & fears

in both cases what it feels like in the body—against the backdrop of war which so threatens it

~ ~ ~

Vancouver Jan. 6. 88

Taken, by surprise—how she was, my mother, on her wedding night
—how she wasn't really, groomed as she was in
feminine "charm"
(ripe for taking?)
—how Singapore was taken, the people taken in by the
colonial govt's belief in its military superiority

talking with Betsy about my dream this morning over breakfast at the Naam [Cafe]: what is the difference between dream logic & the logic of the daily—or how are dreams differently organized?

she said her dreams are more narrative than her writing (but would she say than her life? perhaps more than <u>daily</u> life)—i was suprised, though i think it's true of my escape or problem dreams—they're definitely situational & working towards escape or solution (narrative)—but lots of dreams seem processional, a procession of images, voices, faces without necessarily going anywhere—often the outcome the dream's supposedly working towards is subverted by something else & never arrived at—only desperation, a life-threatening situation, drives my dreamer to such action she explodes the dream

B. commented on how she seems always inside her dreaming, not in control of it—i said that feels like writing, at least the kind of writing we do, which is unplotted & interacts with its medium—the words determine/shape the "drift" just as images & words do in dream—how dream uses everything that comes up, doesn't pick & choose, edit, or "direct"

she said, thinking of Cheryl [Sourkes] & her photographic work, her interest in dreams, i wonder what effect working on <u>white</u> paper has for the writer? if we worked on black (negative) would it change the writing?

is dream the negative of our daytime life? not the reverse, but the coming-into-being, as an image comes into being in the developing tank? developed from traces, bits & pieces of our daytime life collapsed together? (Cheryl's negative collages as traces of her reading)

"Territory & co.":—work with anacolutha as a compositional guide— abrupt changes/transitions within the narrative (not just the sentence) —to surface the latent, the repressed lesbian body beginning to surface in the late 70s with lesbian friends

~ ~ ~

Ana Colutha—(as a "character"? just one in a possible series of names)
—syntactic breaks: ego breaks (Ginsberg in '78: "The ego is not solid.
It breaks all the time. Like in a movie where there are film frames &
then there are gaps in between those frames. Some people think it's
continuous & they try to get into the moving" (direct the plot).

it's the "& co." that has to do with taking apart the ownership &
continuity of ego-territory & its naming

knock-knock jokes for Ana—
                    Ana Colutha
                    Ana M.Nesis
                    Ana Chronistic

to be lost between versions . . . you've lost out . . . to have lost touch
with . . .

Ana Strophe: inversion of the normal (syntactic) order

~ ~ ~

Jan. 12. 88.

early this morning i dream a Keefer St. dream:

                              i'm in the kitchen wearing a hairnet (!) &
apron, one of those old-fashioned aprons with frilly shoulders—i'm
sweeping the floor—Roy's there getting coffee or something— Warren's
walking out the front door with some parting shot at Roy i don't
remember now, friendly but with rivalry in it—bp's arranging something
in the living room, not just furniture, some art project—Betsy comes to

the kitchen & urges me to stop sweeping & walk into the living room with her towards the large window —look, she says, & i see that although we've stopped walking our figures are still walking away together in the window—she's delighted to be showing me—but how? i ask—it turns out to be some complicated arrangement with mirrors that bp has set up behind us—then i look over & see Roy sitting in an armchair & beside him (between his chair & the bookshelf) a strange-looking column made of blue & white swirled styrofoam, like the stuff they make portable coolers with, & on top is crouched a gorgeous blue ceramic celestial dog/lion, the kind that guard the entrance-way to imperial halls—i'm amazed he's made it without my knowing or even seeing—

later this morning when i call Coach House about my proofs Diane Martin tells me that she's just heard that Roy's & Sharon's [Thesen] books have been shortlisted for the GG's this year!—i phone Roy to congratulate him & tell him the dream: it seems annunciatory in some way, even while being the product of reading my '77–'78 journals & all their painful agonizing.

almost forgot, in the dream, in the kitchen before Betsy comes in, i'm saying to myself with surprise, that's right, i'm still married, i can't really be a lesbian then or how did i do this? become a lesbian & still stay in this relationship with a man?

so we walked away, Betsy walked me through the window & i went with her (it wasn't just a trick of mirrors)—& Roy, writing out his pain, made something strange & beautiful & celestial of it all [The Pear Tree Pomes]— i'm so glad they've finally acknowledged his poetry—

    he said, you always did have exotic dreams.

~ ~ ~

Vancouver. March 21. 88.

so why do i still balk at the notion of action? the hero?

early forms of story: adventures for children—i read them avidly, but
except for the *Swallows & Amazons* series they were all boys adventuring
—Jim Hawkins, Tom Sawyer. Alice, yes, but look what happened to her
—those distortions of body-size, distressing transformations—she
<u>suffered</u> her way back home, & all because she was curious

the hero overcomes: that first little book i hand-printed & made drawings
for in Penang: child-ballerina overcomes burglar. forgot this when i asked
Kit (at about the same age) why his play scenarios invariably featured car
chases & crime —his look of withering patience: because it's ACTION of
course! of course—the very stuff of superheroes

but there's a looser kind of narration in journal-writing, the kind that
demonstrates the connection between narration & knowing (both joined
at root by I-E *gno-*, to know)—trying to discern the shape, the repeating
patterns of our lives, a mapping of contours amidst the scatter of the
daily so we can locate ourselves, come to know who we are apart from the
socio-cultural images of who we're "supposed" to be

is conquest the only engaging story-line? what if writing is itself the first
necessary act of resistance, making what we think & feel known to
ourselves? what if the territory we explore (not conquer) is the territory
of gender relations & its scripting in conventional narrative? Teresa de
Lauretis here

~ ~ ~

WOMEN AND NARRATIVE

1. "Narrative is a strategy for survival." (Daphne Marlatt, How Hug a Stone) Is narrative a way of validating your own experience? Is it a way of being/writing the female hero of your own story?

2. What is the social/political responsibility of the writer/ storyteller? When you are writing/telling your story, what is your relationship to your audience?

3. Do you see a difference between male and female narrative? What are the possible characteristics of a narrative "in the feminine"?

4. "There is no such thing as non-narrative writing." (Bob Perelman) How do you deal with narrative expectations? Do you consciously use or subvert (conventional) narrative structure?

5. Do women readers and writers feel the same relation to the ending of the story as men do? A male writer has described the reader's "lust for closure." Is the satisfying conclusion a narrative goal for (heterosexual and lesbian) women? How about the possibilities for what Rachel Blau duPlessis calls "writing beyond the ending"?

6. Who are the voices and the subjects speaking in women's narrative? Are they silent elsewhere?

Old Scripts and New Narrative Strategies

In the spring of 1988, Julie Emerson of the Vancouver Women and Words Society, organized a series of public panel discussions on issues of feminist writing. For the discussion on women and narrative, she brought writers Gladys Hindmarch and me together with theorist Susan Knutson and storyteller Nan Gregory.

"Narrative is a strategy for survival."

This statement, plucked out of the air one day, seems to resonate not only for me but for others. I literally did catch it on the airwaves, a fragment of a CBC conversation on my car radio, overheard while running errands one frenetic day in 1982. I had no idea who said it, but it stayed with me and eventually worked its way into the Avebury poem in *How Hug a Stone*. Now it appears in the guise of a quote from that poem as a point of reference for our discussion of women and narrative. Let's call this a continuing instance of immediate recognition, when an old given (narrative) suddenly makes new sense in a different context and with a different kind of hearing.

That anecdote is itself a micro-narrative which illustrates the survival of a particular string of words, a sentence, a making-sense. The sentence survives because it intimates something about collective strategy, about how we as women come to tell our own stories, which may then resonate for others and so survive beyond the particulars of our immediate lives.

Any story, no matter how small, participates in larger cultural ones that to some extent determine it. The larger culture's narratives perpetuate cultural assumptions, if not obviously (as in creation myths or biblical parables) then covertly in how these stories are told. Without thinking about this, we tell stories every day to make our lives real to ourselves and our intimates. After all, to narrate is to tell the happenings of (in sequence): this happened to me, then this, or, she said, then i said. . . . it's how we come to know the shape of our lives and perpetuate what is important to us. For at the root of *narrating* is *knowing*, embedded in Indo-European *gno-* and later in Latin *gnarus*, a word which means knowing, expert.

The difficulty for us as women has been that our most important cultural narratives (the scriptures, heroic tales, official histories, legal judgements and classic stories our culture hands down to us) were largely invented by male experts who gave us stories to live by and images of ourselves to live up to (good girl, devoted wife and mother), as well as images of a fate to avoid (slut, harpy, lunatic). Many feminist critics have commented on the fate of women characters in eighteenth- and nineteenth-century novels, how there were only two roads to choose between: either you were virtuous and protected in the "bosom" of the family (nurturance was definitely your task, your value), or you rebelled and were cast out on your own, left unprotected and devalued. When the conventional female script meant nurturing the heroics of others, what did it take for a woman to write her own script, conceive of herself as the positive hero of her own life story?

We learned that heroines were the female counterparts of heroes, but we also learned the popularly trivialized associations of that term. The heroine, as often as not, was the woman who escaped harm and not through her own actions but through the agency of others—tied to the rail of advancing locomotives, stalked through dark alleys, enduring accident after accident, she is "saved" in the nick of time by the hero. If heroes are protectors and heroines all too often the protected, then how can women undertake their own quest, how can they "sally forth" (yes, with their female names) into unknown territory, become, as Audrey Thomas asks in *Intertidal Life*, the explorers?

There is a previously little-known territory which women began to explore and name in this century, the territory of gender relations and its scripting in conventional narrative. These explorations might even be called "heroic" because it is always most difficult to name the unnamed, the implicit, to foreground the previously unseen background.

Teresa de Lauretis ("Desire in Narrative") provides some useful insight into narrative and the conventional nature of heroics. She asserts that narrative functions to map differences, especially and perhaps primarily sexual difference. This mapping occurs in two mythical positions: the boundary-space through which the hero passes on his quest and his heroic passage which is the movement of the story—after all, the hero's story is never the monster's, is certainly never seen from the perspective of those he conquers. The monsters he overcomes and the places through which he passes are female elements which simply mark his positions in the story, and they are seen from *his* point of view as mere background to his exploits or as passing threats to his selfhood (in short, womb = tomb, the mother the boy-hero fights free of in order to prove his manhood).

So if this is the traditional narrative we grew up with, the supposed script of reality, you can see it doesn't have much to say about women's passages, about our own narratives of developing selfhood or a woman-oriented sense of reality. What happens when the monster tells her own story? (The question Jean Rhys answered in *Wide Sargasso Sea* with its inversion of the monsters.)

In our various ways we are revising the old scripts, reversing them. For how can what we write *not* be a reversal when we foreground women's perspective? when the background assumes a speaking voice? The cave speaks, the desert sings and the unexamined world which was merely background for his exploits suddenly becomes so live, so resonant with alternative givens, there is no longer any sure footing in the old order of things. What happens to the hero then?

A woman narrator who turns the world upside down as she explores it (i don't want to call her a hero, because hero implies a singular line of relating, his), such a woman narrator has a well-grounded distrust of the heroics of exploit. That is why i think and hope we won't simply change the gender of our heroes but subvert them, subvert the whole exploitive business of the singularly heroic and with it the distorting effects of monocular point of view. For the selfhood that women's texts narrate is not a heroic selfhood that overcomes, so much as a multi-faceted one (if indeed it can be called *one*) that stands in relation to all that composes it—of necessity complicit with, and necessarily refusing, the protector-protected script of what Adrienne Rich calls "compulsory heterosexuality," that old script of gender opposites and opposition. Feminist writing reaches for something beyond the notion of conquest, romantic or not. It undoes oppositions in a multivalent desire for relationship, whether with women or men, children, cats, trees, the particular slant of light in a street or a breaking wave, a certain luminosity of being (as Virginia Woolf would put it) we participate in.

Our reaching across what divides us in class, race and religion, our continual questing for what we share, even as we refuse to elide our differences for the sake of a "unified voice"—all this is subversive of the old script of oppositions. As daughters of our mothers, and particularly as lesbian daughters of our mothers, we stand in a curious relation to that script because we were raised with it. I often feel—not *complicit* perhaps, so much as *duplicit* or double. Even as i try to divest myself of its confining traces i feel how they enfold me still in the culture at large (after all i came to my sexuality inside its seductions). So my subversion takes the form of re-vising from the inside, not so much stepping out of old clothes as seeing through them, seeing through the ways it's possible to still hide in them. Perhaps it's the effort of this seeing-through, this "re-vising" to quote Rich again, that tends to make women's narrative autobiographical. And coiling in its movement, nesting in on itself even as it grows outward into a newly perceived world.

In 1985, at the New Poetics Colloquium in Vancouver, Nicole Brossard pointed out that writing is so important for women because through it we become visible in public space. And in establishing our own individual territory in our writing, each of us creates more public space for other women to inhabit. I think this is true and terribly important. And it seems to me that the public space women come to inhabit, while it may be visible for others, is crucially for ourselves an aural one, a space resonant with words that speak to us. For readers as well as writers, narrative can be a strategy for survival. In the sharing of narrative, an audience becomes less an audience of spectators than an audience of *hearers*. We hear each other out, we actively relate what another woman is saying to our own experience, and that moment of rapport comes when there is sudden recognition of a heretofore silenced reality we share.

68

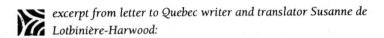 *excerpt from letter to Quebec writer and translator Susanne de Lotbinière-Harwood:*

Vancouver. January 20. 89

it's impossible to translate a piece in its entirety (i mean both the sound-body of the text as well as the aura of meaning that radiates or resonates off the denotative body of the text)and as you know—& every translation can only be a reading (the translator makes certain choices another translator would not). so i thought of my "translation" or "transformance" as an intimate reading that played not merely with denotation, but with sound, & with that subtle aura of meaning-resonance.

because i lived with Nicole's text for weeks, discussing it with several friends, reading & re-reading, tracing through levels of "mauve"—yes, it definitely has a mauve "aura"—in that intimacy i began to want to respond to the poem, on its own terms or at least on extensions of those terms. so that's what the coda does: it comments on the process of reading both the lines & between the lines of Nicole's poem, on that exchange of "sense" which spreads like a stain from the thinking tissue of the writer to the perceiving tissue of the reader—who is also thinking her way through the intimate play of "putting it all together."

Nicole's work is a challenge to translate because it demands that kind of intimacy of thought, that kind of idea-transfusion in the branching veins of language.

~ ~ ~

Translating *MAUVE*

At the 1988 Association for Canadian and Quebec Literatures Conference in Windsor, in a panel discussion titled "Translating Each Other" organized by Kathy Mezei, Nicole Brossard and I talked about the project of "transformance" in our two chapbooks, MAUVE (her poem, my translation) and Character/Jeu de Lettres (my poem, her translation), which had been jointly published by Writing magazine in Vancouver and La nouvelle barre du jour in Montreal. The following appeared in Tessera 6 (spring 1989), an issue on feminist translation.

Translation stands in an intimate relationship to writing. Unlike writing, it works from an original "score," but like writing it requires creative play to come off the page live in another language, a different performance. The shades of difference between faithful but dead imitation and live performance can be fascinating. And it is exactly this area of difference—i might even add this "shady" area—that the process of translation works.

As i write this, i'm assailed by words like "accuracy" and "basis" (proper), which want to insert themselves, but what i want to say about translation denies those terms. Translation is about slippage and difference, not the mimesis of something solid and objectified out there. Even though i begin with a text that is another's, how i read that text or what that text seems to be saying will occur in an indeterminate space between its author's vision and my own: this is not the text i would have written, but it is the text that i am reading and, in a dubious sense, rewriting. Dubious because nothing is decided ahead of time. What i write will be the result of the very elastic play between all that the poem might be saying and what i come to hear, complicated by the shift between the poem's play of meaning in its original French and what it comes to mean in the slightly different verbal play of English. Since it is impossible to "bring over" all of the complex of meaning in French, this difference is crucial. And fascinating. And a clear instance of what writing itself is about: sensing one's way through the sentence, through (by means of) a medium (language) that has its own slippage of meaning, its own drift. So that what one ends up saying in the poem is never simply one with, but slipping, in a subtle displacement of, authorial intention. Meaning is the poem's complex issue, both what i thought to say and what language brings into play beyond my intention.

If writing involves this kind of slippage, then translation involves it even more, since there are two minds (each with its conscious and unconscious), two world views, two ways of moving through two different languages. All of this is compounded when you have two women writers aware of the displacement that occurs between their own experience as woman and that drift that is patriarchally loaded in their language. Then you have both drift and resistance, immersion and subversion—working together.

Given all this, i was delighted when Colin Browne asked me to translate a poem by Nicole Brossard for the new series he and Michel Gay were inaugurating in a joint publishing venture between *Writing* and *NBJ* (*La nouvelle barre du jour*). It was to be a series of "transformances," he said. How could, or even would, i refuse when the definition of transformance he gave me included "reading, writing, writing reading—that flicker pan-linear, lured beyond equivalence: a new skin . . ." especially when it was the author of "Tender Skin My Mind" i would be translating.

When i first received the pages of *MAUVE* with their four elliptical poem-statements, i went into despair: how translate these hermetic instances of poem/theory so unfamiliar in their philosophic and perceptual concerns to anything in the English tradition? Meaning operates strangely in them, seeping from one phrase to others around it, leaking back and forth between fragments, definitely not progressing in linear fashion. The last poem ends with the leap:

> fiction culture cortex
> M   A   U   V   E

Spaced out mauve, a mauve i kept turning over in my mind, trying to perceive its various verbal hues, clues. Here was a marvellously untranslatable word, a truly bilingual word that transferred nothing but itself. Mauve is mauve, and also, like a rose in English, a mauve is a flowering plant in French—mauve is a mauve is a mauve. It's not that the spiral stops here but that it circles back and stains everything leading up to it with its semantic colour.

Throw the stone of an untranslatable word into the fluent drifts of culture, into "fiction culture cortex," and it ripples out: roseblue, or "bluer and paler than monsignor" (*Webster's*), or the colour of rebellious women, secret code of lesbians say Judy Grahn and Dale Spender, insisting on its history (Mauve, eh? mauvais!)—the colour of a bruise, connected with violence and also vision in *L'Amer* ("L'Acte violent de l'oeil au mauve épris s'infiltre ravi déployant"), the smitten purple we see by, converting light into electrical impulses, into the language of the nervous system. A woman's colour, uncontainable, signalling seepage and desire, transgression of boundaries, connection, communication.

Talking about the poem after translating it, i seem to be working backwards through it, though translating it i worked forwards. This seems analogous with the working of the poem as a whole, its end implicated in its beginning. A kind of doubling works throughout and at the start most obviously with mouths, their relationship to another double, reality and the real, even as they double each other. Curves of the mouth resembling the images that surround us in a reality that is not the real, "La bouche au féminin," that mouth which speaks of another real and another (dorsal) mouth—the slippage between the social medium and the subjective one, like the displacement (the curve) of something going underwater. Nicole's lines make this curve, making leaps of displacement between the living body and its mental impress, the divergence of the virtual, especially from the point of view of woman whose body is much imaged: a paradigm for that difference between writing and the written.

There is the horizon line of language which represents the edge thought comes to, and then there is the leap beyond that borderline of words, beyond the edge of the page, which i came to see as a leap beyond the separateness of two languages, two minds. For, paradoxically, it is through language which separates us that meaning flowers in the brain, seeping like a bruise from one mind to another in a transgression of limits. Translating MAUVE became a remarkable performance of this process, a reading of the depths of the drift suggested by Nicole's minimal lines on the page—i felt, in the process, as if my own cerebral cortex were being marked or written on.

I came to see the final line of letters reading MAUVE, then, as the horizon line of thought indicating that point where meaning curves— beyond it is space resonant with implication. Taking liberties, i wrote a coda to honour this erotic transgression of borders, corporeal, cultural and linguistic, where meaning seeps through the poem from one mind to another. This is a fiction, yes, but it carries an element of truth, like my etymological shift from *malva* (mallow) to *maiwa* (gull or mew riding that horizon line between two elements). Under Nicole's concluding *MAUVE* my reflecting *MAUVE* begins the shift into a shared "cortex fiction culture" which is the inverted continuity of her "fiction culture cortex" (or core-text). It stands as evidence of that stain her meaning leaves in the reader's brain tissue/text (embodying her own hidden play: corps/text, the body as text). Perhaps this is the kind of reading tender women's minds make for each other, slipping the borderlines of skin and sense, playing with that subtle displacement difference is—phonetic, syntactic, metonymic. In this we have a lesbian version of the kind of transport translation can be.

CHERYL SOURKES

Sharon Thesen, Louky Bersianik, Daphne Marlatt, and Louise Cotnoir at the
Women and Words Conference, 1983.

CHERYL SOURKES

Nicole Brossard, Mary Meigs, and Beth Brant at the Women and Words
Conference, 1983.

ALEXANDRA CHARLTON

l-r Betsy Warland, Josee Michaud, and Victoria Freeman at the Women and Words Conference, 1983.

ROBYN ELPHICK

Penn Kemp at the Women and Words Conference, 1983.

ROBYN ELPHICK

Phyllis Webb and Margaret Atwood at the Women and Words Conference, 1983.

ALEXANDRA CHARLTON

Susan Knutson, sound technician at the Women and Words Conference, 1983.

LORRAINE OADES

Dorothy Livesay at the Women and Words Conference, 1983.

Sarah Sheard at the Women and Words Conference, 1983.

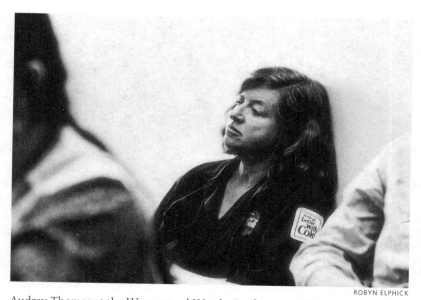

Audrey Thomas at the Women and Words Conference, 1983.

DANI WOOD

Louky Bersianik at the Women and Words Conference, 1983.

CORAL ARRAND

Nicole Brossard reading at the Women and Words Conference, 1983.

ROBYN ELPHICK

Phyllis Webb at the Women and Words Conference,
1983.

Unmaking/Remaking Poetry in Her Many Images

At the close of 1987 Marguerite Andersen wrote from the Institute for the Study of Women, at Mount Saint Vincent University in Halifax, to tell me that she and Melanie Randall were planning a Canadian women's handbook, "a sort of feminist encyclopedia" (which unfortunately never reached publication). She asked me to contribute something on the changes women were making in poetry, which gave me the opportunity to assemble a sort of feminist poetry newsflash.

Poetry, that inspired making (*poiein*) with words, that wellspring, that temple of the oracular, that lyric construction of the exalted I —women come to it troubled, doubled by the graven/craven images men have provided: Eve of the forked tongue, miss-represented, ma-damned. "Maker" a word for God (how dare she?): a word for poet, female.

Women have dared for a long time. But at issue in Canadian feminist poetry in English today are the terms of that daring. Women who write are "coming to," leery of His naming, wanting to find other words for what we see slipping between the lines, fading into the void of women's non(re)presentable desire. "What does woman want?" That blindsided Freudian question assumes a new resonance.

For one thing, not to be *she*-seen but *I*-seeing, not beside herself, a freakish she caught in her own reflection, but I + I, makes we, political. To put words to what this I sees, to soar on collective wings, find language that will lift us onto the page in a polylogue of our own making. But what language? And how do we write our way out of a tradition that tells us our actual experience is not the stuff of poetry?

Stuff is what it's about (a plug, a cork). Pulling it out of our ears, we come alive in a verbal universe, *perfectly musical / / and coloured enough, though featherless, / for a kind of flying* (Webb 19). Taking issue (yes, and exit-ing tradition) with language, genre and symbol, women are coming to poetry not to be made in it but to make it, remake it in light of our own vision—*because in the small womb / lies all the lightning* (Livesay 108).

And unmaking it, we make fun, poking polysemic holes in the mono-lithic: *Ma jerks / magic off / the gram / off the grammer / phone* (Kemp 6). Or making it up as we go along, reinventing, reassembling the left out bits of knowledge we've had since we were children, *finding the child provoked, invoked, lost daughter, other mother and lover* (Marlatt, *Touch*, 27). Reinterpreting the old tales: *Watch yourself. That's what mirrors are for, this story is a mirror story which rhymes with horror story* (Atwood 52).

Sounding the words that echo obsessively in the mind, making them count, making them what we value, bodies (of work) that record —*I want nothing that enters me / screaming / claiming to be history* (Brand 26).

Indeed we have been counting all our lives, skipping early on the (false) line, scotching categories that would contain us—*my heart consistently shatters in the frame of your reference* (Fitzgerald 43). We know what gender-destiny is: *Mary is my mother & her favourite / colour is blue* (Brandt 31). Boundary-runners crossing the genre-line

—*sometimes you can't tell where the bird's lungs / end & the sky begins* (Mouré 77)—crossing poetry with prose, the mundane with the mythic, trying to open up the unspoken, *while the strictures of the lyric / huddle in the aether / fumbling with matches, trying / to do something with language* (Thesen, *Beginning,* 43).

This language women struggle with, to speak, through its universality, its silencing, the immediate and particular realities of gender, race and ethnicity—*a foreign anguish / is english.* (Philip 58).

The news is that women are making news, remaking the new in the frightful imagery of a real we see with our own eyes, seeing *the planet destroyed / if necessary / life / / for the supremacy / of an economic / theory* (Harris 40). We are seeing through the cover stories—*do not be deceived by appearances / I am not a woman I am a sequence / dismembered* (Lemire Tostevin, *Double,* n.p.). Satirizing the transcendental signifier which has made history—*He does not yet have a piece of his brain / in the head of his penis,* the mother says of the little boy (Scheier 28). In short, women poets are un-writing *man-made manologue* (Warland, *Serpent,* n.p.) to create an altered *AUTHORITY. ANOTHERITY* (Warland, *Serpent,* n.p.)—to make good our word finally on our own terms.

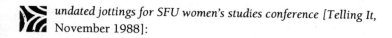 *undated jottings for SFU women's studies conference [Telling It,* November 1988]:

opportunity to feature women writers from marginalized communities that don't usually get represented in such conferences—make it non-academic—at intersection of writing & political activism—to celebrate the writing but also generate strategies in common

writers from 3 different groups:
> Native community
> Asian-Canadian community
> & lesbian community

what are the cross-over lines? rift lines?

lesbian community crosses over into the other 2 but is also discriminated against as a specific group in the mainstream—has its own underground cohesiveness, cultural codes, humour, gathering places

difficult for ethnic writers to come out as lesbian within their communities? —but then what about subtle race-discrimination within the feminist lesbian community?

racism & homophobia the double rift-lines—not only without but also within each community—

feature certain themes in panel discussion: what is the writer's relationship to her audience? at large? in each community? how does writing reflect politics? function of storytelling (oral & written) in a community?

> —won't work unless we can throw it open
somehow—essential to get input from speakers themselves abt what's important to talk about

~ ~ ~

re-reading Barbara's piece ["Becoming my Hero, Becoming Myself"] which covers so much reader-theory ground so succinctly:

she talks about the woman reader "attempt[ing] to create herself as a male in order to become her hero" (she read *Swallows & Amazons* as a child too!)—that desire to scale cultural fences, break limits, dodge one's "fate" as a girl—then moving on to become the resisting reader who deliberately "misreads" the old plots where she's supposed to be the object of his attention instead of the subject of her own story—then she moves on to what seems to me truly feminist, reading empathetically, "an intersubjective reading with the heart and mind of another woman" (nice phrase!)

—here she talks about the danger of MERGING or "losing oneself in the other," which strikes home in a way it didn't before B[etsy] & i began our collab. about collaborating ["Between the Lines"]

—yes, the danger of being subsumed in an over-riding "we" which erases the actual differences between "you" & "me"—reflects the problem the feminist movement as a whole is facing, the recognition that "we" is mostly specific to the speaker, & exclusive

in our "we," B's & mine, is my fear of being spoken for just a reflection of the competitive individualism we've been steeped in? & if so, how put that together with our desire as lovers to enact a "we"? <u>do</u> 2 women lovers collaborating run a greater risk of merging? or does that question itself reflect a sort of internalized homophobia?

Barbara ends with all-important context, how different the contexts are that each of us brings to reading and writing—their <u>specificities</u> so crucial here: how recognizing them leads to notions of real exchange—rather than private monopoly (& feelings of deprivation)

~ ~ ~

Intro. to "Subverting the Heroic"

So much women's writing in BC. — talk about the (Yuk
sm by writers who ~~who~~ see themselves as feminist
of an analysis in their work — around language, ~~you~~
hegemony of certain ~~particular~~ storylines
own (40's & early 50's) but even so still left out
. a different relationship to their audience than feminist do — feminist writers have a certain re-
that is based on mutual recognition ~~of certain~~ (an
I write undertaken in the work — this means that there is
an. That is particular to this relationship (talk about

of this paper ~~first~~ for me was taking very different wh-
a what they have in common in their writing — i mean a
commitment to write for a feminist perspective (c
iderably in terms of what it embraces) — a to see p
of concern, even strategies, in common.
. in the writing which all are only just becoming aware of, a
see Moraille
lily being done by native writers (like Jeanette Armstrong

Subverting the Heroic in Feminist Writing of the West Coast

In May of 1988 the Regional Women's Studies Conference on Bowen Island, organized by the programme at Simon Fraser, brought together women's studies faculty from universities and community colleges throughout B.C. and the Yukon. Veronica Strong-Boag, then chair of the programme at SFU, asked me to speak on contemporary women's writing in the region, and later included the essay in a collection she edited with Gillian Creese: British Columbia Reconsidered: Essays on Women.

In this most western of provinces at the edge of the continent, we live in a culture not yet disengaged from its frontier roots. Pioneers, that laudatory word for invasive settlers, means something quite different on the coast than it does on the prairies. Our pioneers were less homesteaders than bushwhackers, goldpanners, brothel-keepers, drovers, drifters—men and women on the move, self-reliant, daring, opportunistic. We still live in the macho culture of frontier heroism they bequeathed to us. In this culture, art of any kind has little value because it doesn't contribute in an obvious way to survival. In fact, the ways in which art does contribute to the survival of a moral and spiritual vision larger than rugged individualism, or the ways in which it contributes to a sense of cultural community, are publically undervalued. This makes for a difficult environment for writers of either gender and it makes it doubly hard for women—who have never figured as cultural heroes in the macho scheme of things—to write out of a distinctively female ethos and vision.

Yet British Columbia is home to a number of women writers who have been successfully doing so for years: Dorothy Livesay, Jane Rule, P.K. Page, Phyllis Webb, Audrey Thomas, to name only a few, not to mention literary fore-mothers like Ethel Wilson and Emily Carr. How account for this abundance given such rock-hard soil? Perhaps like the arbutus, also known as Crazy-Woman Tree, we thrive in opposition to the norm, drop our leaves when we're not supposed to, shed our bark and still flower. Frontier heroism, with its cult of the macho individual who beats all odds to survive, has paradoxically provided ground for an alternative feminist vision which is not only rewriting the old heroic script but changing our cultural values as it challenges the language in which the old values are embedded.

I want to talk about this in light of a handful of recent books by a generation of women writers in their forties and early fifties whose writing is marked by a feminist resistance to the romance of heroism as well as to the aesthetic norms that convey that romance. Their writing challenges notions of the conventional lyric or conventional forms of the novel just as it rewrites the old heroic script with its inscribed gender roles.

In this script, the stereotypical hero is bent on rescuing innocent women (damsels in distress) or defeating experienced women (witches, monsters, evil seductresses). The woman's role is secondary; she is either the reward for the successful completion of his quest or the threat he overcomes. Not much of a role in either case. During a Women and Words panel on narrative in Vancouver (April 1988), a woman suggested that if the story of St. George and the Dragon were to be told from a woman's perspective, she would have to be the dragon, since that was the only role that allowed her any action. In fiction women have largely had their destinies determined for them, by happy (or not so happy) accident and by other characters. How many stories written from a woman's point of view, even from the point of view of a woman trying to achieve her own destiny (read selfhood), end with her giving it all up to marry the hero? Conquered by love again, to use a phrase from Harlequin romances.

Paulette Jiles, in an article titled "In Search of the Picara," complained about this cultural script as a "dependency melodrama" (32) that haunts fiction by women. Heroine as appendange of ("-ine" indicating leg or arm perhaps? certainly something belonging to) the hero. Jiles calls for a new leading character who is not ladylike and consequently has full use of her own legs and arms, namely the picara. Unlike the heroine who never initiates action but is merely acted upon, the picara would be the centre of a sequence of events she herself sets in motion. She "takes action because she must" (34).

This would certainly describe Anne, one of the central characters of Anne Cameron's *The Journey*, a novel which blends picaresque western and domestic romance. Here the picaras are two female outcasts who overcome an astonishing array of threats, setbacks, and psychological inhibitions to treck westward at the turn of the century and set up house together as lovers and mothers of an odd assortment of children in a log cabin on the coast. *The Journey* is a female western inhabited by the usual western characters—prostitutes and madam, lynchmob and marshall, drovers and settlers—but its real heroes are women who overcome the male brutality and exploitation they have been victimized by. The kind of survival they seek is psychological, the integration of a healthy and independent female psyche, one that is at home in its environment in a most western way.

The only conquering going on here is the conquering of the dependency syndrome.

For another look at the word heroine, and a different coining, I would like to turn back to a classic of contemporary feminist literary criticism, Ellen Moers' *Literary Women*. Moers talks about an age of "heroinism" when literary feminism first came into print with the writing of women in the late eighteenth and nineteenth centuries. She defines heroinism as "a massive force for change in literature" (189) and as "that feminine enterprise of rousing the imagination 'to a vision of human claims' in races, sects, and classes different from the established norm" (59). Writing from their marginalized position, women were identifying with other marginal and colonized groups. They wrote for the abolition of slavery, they called for women's education and the right to vote, they wrote about women's poverty and powerlessness. In short, they had a well-developed sense of the larger possibilities of community. Cameron carries on this tradition in *The Journey* as Anne and Sarah, in their struggle for survival, help other victims of the same brutality they have experienced: escaping Chinese coolies, neglected children of a white-trash settler, a raggedy man on the run from a morality-crazed marshall.

The women writers of Moers' "age of heroinism" were middle class and privileged with enough leisure to write and some form of education (even though it was inferior to that of men). Yet many of them were trying to speak for other underprivileged and silenced women. Today more and more women are writing out of their own marginalized experience, working-class writers like Helen Potrebenko, Native and other writers of colour like Lee Maracle and Sky Lee. The directness and immediacy of these once-silenced voices create another subversion of the heroic and its romantic heightening.

Helen Potrebenko's poems, which speak of and with the repetitiveness of most women's office jobs, have a deliberate flatness that runs counter to the lyric tradition, yet they are close to the oral roots of poetry and some of them read like songs to be sung on a picket line. She often refers ironically to pop culture, as in the title "It's a Bird; It's a Plane . . . / No, It's . . . Supertemp" (*Life*, 47), which deliberately feminizes Superman and conflates a temporary and tedious office job with his heroic pursuits.

This conflation of the mundane and the heroic resonates throughout Potrebenko's poetry, and perhaps most strikingly (no pun intended) in "Days and Nights on the Picket Line." The speaker in the poem adds up all the miles she's walked in circles as a picketer, this activity in its monotonous repetition evoking that generically female activity, housework, which has never been (could it ever be?) seen as heroic. She takes these circular miles and lays them out in linear fashion to indicate where she would have got to by now if she'd been walking in a straight line heroically across Canada. After all, the heroic always involves a goal, the attainment of something. Just think, she says,

> The walking I did on anti-war marches
> would have got me to Abbotsford;
> the Cunningham boycott,
> to Chilliawack.
> If I hadn't walked in front of the Medieval Inn,
> or Wardair,
> I could have been in Hope.
>
> (*Walking*, 6)

By the time she's reached the end of the poem, she's imagining Newfoundland. "I've always wanted to visit Newfoundland, / walking slow" (*Walking*, 8). Playing on the usual values attached to what is heroic or unheroic activity, what is effective or futile action, she wryly pokes fun at the notion of achieving a goal even as she exaggerates the unarriving miles she's walked on picket lines—no small achievement, the poem says.

Anne Cameron has coined another feminized word for heroic action by women in her poem, "Sea Fair, Powell River." She asks us whether we know that hero is a term men stole for themselves from "the goddess Hera / 'the holy one' 'the Earth' / 'the mother of the gods' the ruler / of the apple-orchard of immortality" (*Life,* 105). The poem begins:

> You don't get many chances to see heroism first hand
> It's not as if there were knights chasing dragons or
> crusaders fighting infidels or brave stands to be taken
> in defense of freedom, god, flag, motherhood, and
>   blackberry pie
> All the mountains around here have been climbed,
>   clear-cut logged,
>   eroded, wasted, raped, and desecrated. . . .
>
> <div align="right">(<i>Life,</i> 103)</div>

She goes on to describe standing in a lineup for food with her woman lover, surrounded by that flaunting of macho strength that loggers' sports are all about, when she is taken aback to hear her lover begin, in a loud voice, to air her views on child rape. Everyone around them gets uncomfortably silent, but when she says that she's heard "that the guys who fuck children have penises so small only a kid would be impressed," other women in the line slowly begin to express their own rage and ridicule. "You know it for what it really is when five foot three / stands up to six foot two and names what everyone knows / and nobody discusses," the poem comments and concludes, "Even small Heraisms / are a big deal. Or ought to be" (105).

This renaming of the heroic, this running counter to the usual definitions sanctified by patriarchal culture, is intensified in Betsy Warland's long poem *serpent (w)rite*. In this book she traces the devaluing of the feminine in our culture and in our language back to that original apple-orchard and

> Eve standing beneath the Tree
> with a need in her breast
> something missing in *paradise, per-, (around), pri-*
> *mordial, price, experience, interpret, viper, separate,*
> *fear, postpartum*
> a longing for
> > words
> Adam's naming not an ending
> more words wanted out
> words which spoke of *experience, interpreted* perception
> words of discourse

> > > (n.p.)

Eve and Pandora perform the Heraic actions of resisting prohibition and doing what they must: "taking the bite opening the lid," for which they will be "damned for *opening, upo, evil* / their *lid, klei, clitoris* / / the body condemning the body condemned the body lost." It is through constellations of similarly related words, at times going back to their common root, that Warland generates meaning. Tracing linguistic relationships, she shows how, hidden deep in the history of our aggregate language (further back than the story of creation itself), certain concepts are related and these relationships still function, if subliminally, like scraps of cultural memory. Slowly she pieces together verbal bits of a new version of the story:

> Eve at the crux of the *matter,*
> *mother, matrix, matrimony, material, Demeter*
>
> De-mater
>
> 'De is the delta, or triangle, a female-genital sign
> known as "the letter of the bulba" in Greek sacred
> alphabet'
> > Walker
>
> > > (n.p.)

In the sweep of this book-length poem, Warland moves from Adam and Eve to the arms race and reproductive technology, tracing pervasively negative attitudes towards the body, particularly the female body. In what it takes issue with, much of this poem "names what everyone knows / and nobody discusses," and in its encyclopedic piecing together of quotes from a range of sources, in its leaping from word lists to lyric chant to pointed punning, it is scarcely recognizable as a poem. Yet this transformation of conventional form often goes hand in hand with rewriting the old script.

Take Audrey Thomas's reshaping of the novel. Like Warland, Thomas has a fascination with language and her novels are sprinkled with verbal jokes, bits of wordplay, imaginative deconstructions. Because she works with fiction, she is concerned with narrative, but like Warland's way of progressing through *serpent (w)rite*, her novels tend to move in circles, worrying away at a central emotional snarl to be undone. In her recent novel, *Intertidal Life,* that snarl involves a complex of emotions Alice Hoyle must undergo when her marriage falls apart and she is left alone on an island with three daughters to raise, a book to write and very little money. This snarl that the narrative line has become in Thomas's work subverts the linearity of the usual romance with its progression through conflict to climax and a satisfying end. Her narrative is clogged with the daily, a sticky web of memory, domestic chores, fraught friendships and the litter of a writer's mind endlessly fascinated with quotes, allusions, clippings and bizarre jokes. In fact, Thomas seems to be saying, there is no way out (there is no climactic achievement) except by way of this web, learning to live with it and to love one's messy and multi-faceted self so caught up with it all. The novel is permeated with images of small things that "hang on," limpets, barnacles, species of intertidal life that survive crashing high tides as well as periods of being left high and dry. The periodic repetition of tides is like the oscillation of Alice's moods as she fluctuates between the despair of her "dependency melodrama" and a growing sense of pleasure in her independence and ability to take care of herself and her children. No small achievement given the romantic stereotypes that surround her in the Harlequin romances she and her daughter read or in her husband's desperate quest for a romantic ideal, or in the spiritual romanticism of her hippie friends. It's evident to Alice that this romanticism involves "a flabbiness of spirit"— "It was as though they had had the moral equivalent of a stroke" (97). They were passive, conquered (like the heroines of Harlequin romances) by a vaguely childlike notion of love.

Alice herself is fascinated by the early explorers of the coast. She would like to see herself as an explorer, though she can't quite see being "First Mom on the Moon." Somehow "mother" and "hero" don't conflate. That's the trouble with names, with labels, and the baggage they bring. "Women have *let* men define them, taken their *names* even, with marriage, just like a conquered or newly settled region, *British* Columbia, *British* Guiana . . ." (171). Set adrift, out in the world on their own, women "need new maps, new instruments to try and fix our new positions" (171). Perhaps the most essential of these instruments is language, and Alice works at stripping hers of old and outdated associations. In a stripping of "mother," she traces the word's roots through various languages and alternate meanings ("hysterical passion," "lees, mouldiness") to mummy ("body of a human being or animal embalmed for burial"). "Who can see the 'other' in mother?" she plaintively asks (136).

Paulette Jiles performs a similar stripping of the romantic hero and heroine in *Sitting in the Club Car Drinking Rum and Karma-Kola.* In her witty deconstruction of detective fiction, the hero, a skip-tracer, and the heroine, a credit fraud artist, meet on a Via Rail train travelling east across Canada. He is tracking her down, she is fleeing "a low-grade job at a Seattle television news station" (46), dressed in unpaid-for vintage clothes and inventing a new identity for herself, one that emanates wealth, charm, mystery. She'd like to elude the fate of what Jiles calls the usual heroines of detective fiction, "tramps of some utterly enchanting sort . . . rescued and forgiven by the hard-boiled one and made pure again, usually by violence and repentance" (6). In a reversal of this scenario, by the time they reach Montreal she has seduced him into her romance, converted him from his tough-guy life of "crude pursuits and captures" (26).

Much of the narrative is a commentary on the stereotypes that hero and heroine represent and their attempts to escape these frames:

> She will make up her own story in direct contradiction to what was made up for her; that is to be little and grateful and hard-working, to please people, to escape a low-level job by marriage in which she would be hard-working and grateful and diminished into the littlest thoughts and actions that can be managed (24).

He, on the other hand, "makes up his own story as an enhancement of the one that was made up for him; to be large and active, enterprising and heroic. So there you are. This is how they strike each other; like a match and a sandpaper surface" (24).

In their own ways, the hero and heroine are both writers—they have to be if they are to make up their stories as either contradiction to or enhancement of the old gender scripts. She writes imaginary letters while he writes a spoof of rules for operatives of the agency he works for, which she later undermines and adds to. Their rules admit dreams and curses into the reality they come to construct together, as their way out of what has been made up for them. This is "escapist" fiction with a decidedly postmodern twist.

"[O]f all the picaresque characters the one who strikes me as most interesting is the woman writer," Jiles remarks in her essay and goes on to describe her as someone "who insists on time for herself, is goal-oriented, often poor, focused and fairly organized" (35). Admittedly, most women writers are poor. If they have children, they have to be well-organized to find time to write, time for themselves, which they certainly have to insist on. But I suspect that many women writers rarely feel themselves to be "goal-oriented" and "focused." Jiles has obviously had enough of Woolfian prose when she writes, "[t]he picara is never as interior as the Penelope figure. The prose cannot afford to concern itself with inner dialogue, with impressions, with the heroine's sensitive reactions to everything in sight" (35). Yet even her picara, so committed to action, has nightmares and moments of terror, asks herself what she's doing and why and whether it's worth it. Little things, articles of clothing, for instance, loom large. Women's writing has always paid attention to the little things that the heroic through-line of action ignores as background. In women's foregrounding of background, little things loom large because they are seen as intimately connected with larger issues, whether it's Alice Hoyle weeding her garden and wondering about her own death—"mother in the garden, however deeply dug in?" (258)—or Warland discovering, in that more ancient garden where the serpent was damned to crawl in the dust, that "crawl" connects to "gerebh-," source of "grammar," upon which rational discourse with its binary system (noun-verb, woman-man, passive-active) stands.

In an interview with Eleanor Wachtel in *Room of One's Own* , Audrey Thomas comments on the backgrounding of her own and other women's central concerns in conventional fiction: "I'm amazed at this slight antagonism I feel about the fact that I write about mothers with children; it bothers me, it deeply bothers me. . . . I'm so fed up with hearing that . . . you've got to write *War and Peace*, you've got to write this great diorama of history, *The Naked and the Dead*" (45). It's not that contemporary novels by women are unconcerned with history, but often when they come to write historically women novelists write to include that which has been left out of the "great diorama of history"—namely, women's love and friendship and how that supports their resistance to abuse, as in Cameron's *The Journey,* or the historic repression of women and how the silencing of it warps whole family histories, as in Sky Lee's *Disappearing Moon Cafe.*

Lee's novel, not only the first about Vancouver's Chinatown but the first to give a woman's perspective on the effects of both racism from without and gender oppression from within a Chinese-Canadian community, traces the decline of the Wong family through a series of marriages and parallel liaisons over ninety years and four generations. Kae, the narrator, wants to arrive at a "final reckoning" in this account, but because she is also the granddaughter of one of the family's secret liaisons, she is not outside the story she tells. Working through a maze of half-told history—the struggles of her mother and aunt, her grandmother and great-grandmother toward some solution to the misery of their positioning within the repressive family and community circles of Tang People's Street—Kae is also working her way out of their hold on her, the hold of the story with its "heavy chant" of consequences. In coming to write it, she comes to an understanding of language as both the instrument of domination and the key to liberation for women. "The power of language is that it can be manipulated beyond our control, towards misunderstanding. But then again, the power of language is also in its simple honesty" (180).

Continually presenting both aspects, Lee refuses to accept language at face value. Kae's cynical tongue often slips into language plays to poke holes in "the great wall of silence and invisibility we have built around us" (180). Poking fun with words, she transgresses the code even in the telling of the story: "Fong Mei's pregnancy saved her from unnecessary travel (or should I say travesty) in the nick of time" (154).

Addressing the illegitimacy of Fong Mei's pregnancy, she asks the reader, "And how shameless a hussy was she, with this unwholesome fate soon to be hoisted upon her? She being a young woman in perfect health, and as such no doubt vulnerable to the droplets of male potency found teeming in the air from the sneezes of so many over-anxious bachelors around her" (154).

This sardonic, exaggerated voice, characteristic of the narrative, mimics the heroic voice of the classic storyteller even as it undoes all notions of heroism. *Disappearing Moon Cafe,* with its highly fragmented structure that jumps back and forth in time and point of view, is the story "of one individual thinking collectively" (189). Like the others caught up in their own plot-line, Kae does not know the role she is playing inside her story except as she discovers it in the telling.

This processual quality, which counters notions of heroic achievement, marks women's subversion of the "great diorama." It foregrounds relatedness and community rather than rugged individualism and the cult of the hero. And it fosters strategies of resistance, whether outright reversal of the values and gender of the hero, as in Cameron and Potrebenko, or critique of old stereotypes, as in Jiles, or breaking the dominance of a heroic narrative line with digressive but interconnecting circles of wordplay and memory, as in Thomas, Warland and Lee.

en route to Montreal for the Feminist Book Fair   June 15. 88

little surreal pop clouds low over the tan prairie fields, zigzag rivers, the clouds a flock of sheep except for their shadows like blotches of water under them on the landscape

my mind empty, sleep-stupid (only 5 hours last night)—

more clouds, like a wig now on the bald pate of the land

how to live is the question, how to create space, expansive mind, on the up-&-down seesaw of necessity between working (having money & no time to write) & writing (time, but no money to live on)—seems impossible to reach that elusive balance point

* make Thursdays writing days, at least that one day a week, no matter what:
* finish "Territory & co." [*Salvage*]

the challenge is to decompartmentalize, to bring all of the different aspects of my life into play at once—not to leave the writing behind in a solitary act of privacy but keep it open to all that's going on

flying over Lake Superior, high on red wine (the soul also thrives on <u>induced</u> ecstacy from time to time)—reading Mrs. Dalloway—Woolf so exact in her tracing of the shifts of emotions, their sudden turning points—her use of specific detail to convey a mood, the subtly leading "as if" or "like" & then a whole imagined scene or mini-narrative opens up

the sentence Woolf has refashioned for her use seems most hers in the passage of the woman singing outside the tube station—long & sinuous, embracing asides in parenthetical comments, repeating & circling back on itself but always enlarging—whereas when she portrays Septimus' post-war neurosis the sentences are short, almost chopped (he can't feel): Woolf's marvellous syntactic elasticity in relation to her subject—

& her passage on conversion as the sister goddess of proportion (using Bradshaw's moral language to expose his egocentricity): "that Goddess whose lust is to override opposition," who "feasts on the wills of the weakly, loving to impress, to impose, adoring her own features stamped on the face of the populace"—& then sneaking in her own point about the doctor: "offers help, but desires power"

here she's covertly exposing him, but her effort (& it reads so effortlessly) moves towards inhabiting other viewpoints (if only for a moment), other social perspectives, struggling to enlarge not just her sentence but her vision of the real

Montreal. notes from the Fair. June 16

Saturday afternoon Native women's reading:

Luci Tapahonso, Navajo, says "we are different stories to different people"—she talks about the power of memory as a history bank: "it is through the use of memory that we exist today" (as a people)—"we are independent people through the use of our songs & our stories"—

she talks about listening as participating, seeing your place in the story, the framework—which is altered by your own way of seeing it—this is not appropriating so much as sharing—"there is a power in speaking out loud & enunciating what is within us"—

later Dacia Maraini talks about the woman's body held up to us in advertising as a body without memory—we are mutilated by the lack of public memory, she says

Montreal. Book Fair. June 17

Judy Grahn: the work of Maria Gimbutas, her archeology into the culture of women that preceded Sappho—how Sappho was not a unique woman poet, as we remember her, but lived in on an island of women, in a company of women, from which she addressed all creation

of lesbian writers: women are the centre of our story—every time we touch the threads of that story we make possible our reoriginalization— to originate: come into being, tell where you come from—she says that consciousness is a move towards wholeness which involves originating your community—when you're coming out you're changing origin stories & altering consciousness

the lens of lesbianism sees from both an insider & an outsider position— for a many-centred world

Anna Livia—"Greed not Need: Dare to Presume"—greedy for what we haven't got & no one else has, what is yet to be created—so create it —we shouldn't have areas into which even our imaginations can't venture—

Maureen Brady's story of N. Carolina mill: problem of white woman writing about black workers—Audre Lorde's comment: they're your characters —you can't be presumptuous, only wrong

Dale Spender—"women invented the novel as an alternative to patriarchy": a way for women to communicate with & educate each other, transcend their isolation from each other—"everything I know I've learned from novels"

women's publishing: women have seized the means of production, assumed control—"don't let's lose sight of our successes"—against splitting up over issues around which press is better—

print not the valued medium of exchange anymore, computer technology is—that's why women have been given space to publish themselves

Audrey Lorde—energy never wasted so if we don't use our own specific & relative power it will be used by another power: the necessity of struggling for other women's liberation

the recognition of privilege is the first step in making it available for further use by others—& the importance of using it—absorbing without using is a privilege (educational process teaches us to do this)—unless i use my power in the service of what i believe (that all people must be free) then i'm allowing my power to be used by others—

anger: a grid of distortions between peers, its object is change (not the same as hatred)—learning to use the symphony of angers around us in order to move through (with?) them—learning to focus the anger accurately & sharply to bring about change in women's lives

she says our power is to examine & reconstruct the terms upon which we live & work

the expansiveness of her way of looking at what tears us apart—she articulates how it's possible for each woman to activate her difference for the sake of community

~ ~ ~

Vancouver. July 19. 88

Dear Sarah*:

The only way i'm going to write this letter that yours (much enjoyed) has called for, is to do it in bits & pieces. I can't believe how constantly i'm fighting the clock with my new job (snatching a few moments now to write you from my office). First, it was lovely to hear from you & thank you for your response to Ana. Caroline [Guertin, Coach House Press] was wonderful at the Book Fair, taking it around & getting copies to European publishers. I'd steeled myself to do it, but after the first day of wandering around with a copy hidden in hand wondering who to approach, i was relieved to find she was doing it. Now i hear it's sold out already. Hope the press can reprint soon.

Teaching this summer, organizing a writing conference for the Women's Studies Program for late Nov., trying to get everything ready for *Tessera* 5 (our 1st issue on our own, which CHP is going to print), keeping up with my directed readings students, my thesis-committee grad. student, trying to keep up with my own correspondence, let alone write (haven't looked at "Territory & co." for 2 & half months now), as well as getting enough time with Betsy & worrying about Kit who seems to be floundering around without much sense of direction—it's all a bit much. I don't know how academic women do it year after year.

But my class is a joy, or a dream to use DY's [David Young] term. Articulate, congenial, sensitive to the different needs of women in the group, enthusiastic about the novels we're studying, quick to pick up on theory—seductive, in other words. I could almost let myself get sucked into teaching & stop worrying about writing—well, <u>almost</u>. Then i tell myself, listen kiddo, this isn't a usual class. . . .

Later, so much so it's the 21st. Kit's just lost his job working as an interior house painter. A combination of quitting & being fired under a system of bidding he found hard to take—not much room in it for taking

* Sarah Sheard

pride in his work. Colin, his step-brother, is now in Seattle for the rest of the summer & wanting him to join him. They both claim they'll do some temporary labour jobs tho' i don't know how much labouring is actually going to go on. Raising a teenager seems to involve a constant assessment of the realities in any situation: a lot of reality-testing for mom along with limit-testing by son. I shift like a weathervane between feeling i ought to have more faith in him & feeling i ought to be harder-line.

Your last letter sounded as if you've been pretty stretched yourself. Hope that simplifying your time (you were on the edge of abandoning jobs & moving into just mothering & writing) panned out. And that you've had a lovely time at Georgian Bay, you three. And that the second draft of the novel is running smoothly out of your fingertips. It's odd how sometimes abandoning a draft altogether suddenly opens up a much more articulate space—i found that with mine. And then found i could go back & retrieve pieces of the old draft with only a few changes, mostly cuts. Uncertainty always makes me run on in writing whereas it makes me silent socially. Or maybe i should say in fiction—in poetry it tends to stop me short too. But it's so wonderful to hit that groove of the right voice, the one that allows the material to come. Writing this to you makes me want to think forward to the next one, which is only at the stage of little tickles somewhere at the back of my brain. Tantalizing little tickles suggesting so much more.

I've been teaching Rhys' *Wide Sargasso Sea*, Thomas' *Intertidal Life*, Robinson's *Housekeeping*, Morrison's *Sula*, & now we've moved into my *Ana* which they're doing a great job on. Reading is such a complex activity. I've loved teaching all of them, but *Housekeeping* & *Sula* were a joy.

I'm glad you're doing the fiction chair (with Manguel) at CHP—it makes more sense to me that you should do fiction rather than non-fiction. I've just read a lovely ms. by Liz Hay [*The Only Snow in Havana*], her second in a series she's doing. I think she sent the 1st to Coach House & it was turned down. This one is an elegant weave of history, autobiography, poetic imagery—almost a serial poem in prose. I'll suggest she send it to you to look at.

West Word IV begins in 10 days, with Susan Crean & Dionne Brand arriving from To. to teach, & Donna Smyth from N.S. Somehow we're still managing to pull it off each year.

~ ~ ~

August 3. 88.

Hi, Kit*,

it's another gorgeous summer morning. I've just finished watering the garden, & Kim & Larry who've been staying next door at Betty & Anita's while A. & B. holiday on Gabriola just brought over a bowl of blueberries from their picking in Richmond yesterday. It feels like a very Vancouver summer day.

Your telephone bill arrived this morning & it's due August 22, before you get back. So, to avoid getting your phone disconnected, you'd better pay it from Seattle with some of the money your cartooning has earned. I'll enclose your car registration with it—a little packet of business for you!

Roy made the front page of *The Courier* today. Powell Street Festival— remember it? There's a photo of him reading a poem & standing next to his friend Takeo who's playing the shakuhachi with his head in a basket, Roy glancing at him as he reads with those brown-tinted sunglasses & that quizzical look on his face. It's a great photo.

I just saw Larry walk across the backyard to smell our pink lilies, which are in bloom now & so fragrant that when we eat dinner on the patio all you smell are the lilies. Funny, i never mentioned the lilies to you when i was talking about watering & they're a very wonderful part of the garden. So why didn't i? My mind went like this to itself: maybe i didn't think Kit would be interested—instead i talk about other things. But when i'm older maybe i'll write more about lilies. And maybe that's not because lilies grow more important as i get older but because i reveal different sides of

* Kit Marlatt

myself to you as we both get older. And then i wondered about all the letters my mother wrote to me when i was in the States with Alan before you were born & after, when we went back. I wondered what kind of things she left out because she didn't think they'd mean anything to me. And how that gave me a different sense of who she was than who she really was perhaps—you know what i mean?

Anyway, i think this connects with your comment on the phone last night about how Colin & his mom don't have the kind of conversations (especially the worrying kind!) that we do. And i don't want you to just think of me as your worrying mom—though really i don't think you do—not <u>just</u> that anyway!

The In-Between is Reciprocal

The original version of this talk was given in the spring of 1989 as the Ruth Wynn Woodward Women's Studies talk during my year occupying the Woodward chair at Simon Fraser University. It became the inaugural Mary Catherine Patterson Memorial Lecture at Capilano College later the same year.

The Approach to Writing

How do women approach the traditionally male territory of writing? How do i as a woman approach writing? and why does that word *approach* with its tactility (to come near or nearer to, come close) seem crucial to the question?

These questions insist themselves on the peculiar situation of *writing* a *talk*, which would seem to posit a paradox. After all, a talk implies an exchange in person. Talking is what we do together over a cup of coffee, "book talk" or "people talk" or what we talk about, "the talk of the town," or how we fill in time, with "small talk." There's something casual, convivial, something almost trivial about *talk*, which always requires some form of social collaboration and disappears with our breath, except for the shimmer, never reliable, of memory. Whereas *writing*, that culturally privileged activity, is what we do alone, with thought, forethought even. Undisturbed by the give-and-take of exchange, we have the illusion of entering our deepest thoughts on the blank of the page, raising meaning from the void, the dead—o that messianic touch on the typewriter, the computer keys—as if to save our having been here at all from the ephemeral (e-*fem*-eral?) and enter it in perpetuity, immortally present.

But *writing* a *talk* to be given to unknown others?—as if the give-and-take of conversation could obtain in this room i write in, inventing a future room where we coincide long before we actually come together. By definition you will be silent as audience, and i as speaker will be *giving* you a one-way volley of pre-recorded words. There is something uncomfortable about that definition.

So let me try to approach this scene in writing differently (tactilely, hands out like someone feeling her way along an invisible wall). I miss your physical presence, all that non-verbal language going on in the gap between us as you shift in your chairs, cough, sigh distractedly, laugh or listen in a concentrated way. Not only listening, you are each conducting your private, internal conversation, agreeing, rejecting, questioning, comparing with your own experience. I am putting my thought in your presence so to speak.

Why does it seem necessary to approach this situation of writing a talk so physically, just as Hélène Cixous describes speaking in public: "She doesn't 'speak,' she throws her trembling body forward; she lets go of herself, she flies; all of her passes into her voice, and it's with her body that she vitally supports the 'logic' of her speech" (251). The notion of the solitary i alone in a room writing ignores the interplay of all that affects the writing —not only this lemon-yellow room that holds her one morning in early September, not only the window overlooking a mountain ash, its berries vivid against a sky drained of blue, or the Kitsilano alley empty of all but a solitary cat and odiferous garbage cans—but these other less tangible bodies also present at the moment of writing.

So she puts herself in the position of giving the talk, of talking already —even in writing, which is supposedly one-way, she imagines a two-way situation; she calls up *you* to whom she is speaking. And these words, *talk, speak to, listen*, these words that require a you, a potential respondent, are they indications merely of a too-literal turn of mind? Word for word, yes, she is fascinated, this fictional she who is also me and perhaps you, with what the fictional frame (this writing room, this mountain ash, this alley) renders invisible—you i must break the fiction to reach out to, the fiction that writing is removed from its terms of address and its audience.

To write a talk *as if* in the act of talking to you is a form of transgression that delights and insists itself because its fictiveness invokes an alternate reality. These two words, so mobile in reference, depend on who is speaking, who is listening, for definition. As Nicole Brossard puts it,

> until now reality has been for most women a fiction, that is, the fruit of an imagination which is not their own and to which they do not *actually* succeed in adapting. Let us name some of those fictions here: the military apparatus, the rise in the price of gold, the evening news, pornography, and so on. The man in power and the man on the street know what it's all about. It's their daily reality, or the 'how' of their self-realization (*Aerial*, 75).

Thus Brossard passionately and precisely reverses fiction and reality from a feminist perspective, pointing out that what is real to women is often dismissed as fiction under the terms of a patriarchal real, how confusing this i, how crucial for women to articulate women's realities and name the governing fictions for what they are.

And now as Brossard and Cixous enter this space of writing, we move with them into another aerier space not confined by concrete walls: the space of the writing that has gone before. Every piece of writing enters a dialogue, or maybe polylogue, with other texts to which it stands in some relation, overtly or otherwise. Intertextuality invokes a very large conversation as it parallels or opposes, salutes or appropriates or plays with another text. There are all sorts of bodies, including bodies of work, listening in on this writing even as it responds to them.

But why all this talk of listening? this insistence on response? Feminist writing, conscious of itself as *writing* (culturally elevated), is also conscious of its relation to what has been trivialized as "women's talk"—a trivialization that forgets, as Suzanne Lamy has pointed out, how much recognition of the interrelatedness of being goes on in women's talk, how significant that is to our own well-being. Such writing approaches its audience differently. Close up, touching and being touched, approaching silenced or unwritten areas of experience, it is desirous of response, of mutuality with its readers, its listeners-in. The activeness of this listening in, the activeness of a reading that calls for reading between the lines, ends up with a writing between the lines too.

Between the Lines

First women wrote letters privately to one another. Then they wrote novels about the stories in and of their lives that letters recounted, and often there were letters in these novels. First they were writing to each other to make their stories real to themselves in the way that a story is made real when a friend writes back, "how wonderful," "how awful" and "that happened to me too." And when their novels were published they received letters from strangers who said the same thing, who said their stories, the stories of and from their lives, were real and to be taken seriously. And then women's lives entered the public domain.

Sometimes they wrote snatches of their inner lives in journals, diaries, interrupted by the teeming outer life of husbands, lovers, children, houses, relatives and friends, which the writing could never catch up with, could never record in all its fullness. They put the pieces together trying to glimpse a pattern that could be titled "me," this magnetic heart at the centre of a field of busy particles which only another magnetic heart might recognize. This kind of telling is at the heart of women's talk, which is often elliptical, anecdotal and broken, suggestive in what is left unsaid, in blanks an active listener fills in. Sometimes what we experience as real cannot be expressed because it contradicts the accepted real, because it is unspeakable in its violent reality and the words that would speak it without denying it have not been found.

That great writer of the ellipsis, the blank, Marguerite Duras, has said, "Women have been in darkness for centuries. They don't know themselves. Or only poorly. And when women write, they translate this darkness. . . . Men don't translate. They begin from a theoretical plat-form that is already in place, already elaborated. The writing of women is really translated from the unknown, like a new way of com-municating rather than an already formed language" ("Interview" 425). And again: "[W]hat other people call remains. What, from the outside, one might call remains I would call the main thing" (*Woman,* 45). Which signals the very large shift women's writing inaugurates as it turns what has traditionally been considered background into fore-ground, what has been labelled trivial into the central, what has been belittled as personal and feminine into the largely human. This writ-ing takes a one-way concern with death and heroism and transforms it into an inclusive roundabout of life and community.

The conventional script we have inherited, however, still plays out its old narrative in so much of what surrounds us in our culture. In this script the freely enterprising individual (and yes, you did hear that echo of free enterprise, its motive force, competitiveness, driving the "self-made man") achieves success at the cost of others who are sacri-ficed to his aims, his world-view. Western history, like the small-scale history of the (Far) West, is made up of the stories of such heroes. This colonization of the real requires domination and destruction, and we have begun to see that the destruction of others, whether of forests or of peoples, means the destruction of all of us. Women have long been implicated in this process, but many of us have grown tired of participating in a world shaped by the single-mindedness of a domi-nant authoritative will that ignores the interests of the whole.

To translate this into an approach to language: when Betsy Warland writes "thought is collaboration" ("Reading" 83) she is talking about collaborating with language which is not so much a vehicle for thought (with thought at the wheel) as that rather dense medium in which thought swims, meeting some resistance. Not the sort of tool a hero uses (the getaway car, the pen, the gun), for with this approach language will either be forced to his will or will fail him. She, who thanks to her gender is rarely heroic, finds herself in the midst of language as if she had been thrown into the sea. To stay afloat she must learn the duplicity of language, its rip tides, its capacity for double meaning, its ability to say what she didn't know she meant.

Feminist writing keeps moving toward articulating another real, one which is almost unspeakable given the deeply entrenched terms of the conventional "man-made" real that daily occupies us. But this intuition of another real is communal, responsive, spiraling between and beyond the lines of the entrenched as it tries to open up a space for the speaking out of what has been repressed, erased, demeaned and stripped of meaning. Because this intuition flashes in the realm of the unadmitted, when it seeks to articulate itself it sometimes takes leaps of imagination, sometimes its syntax breaks down, often it freely associates as it collapses habitual meaning, finding kith and kin at the heart of a relating that is telling. It questions what is given—why kith *and* kin, as if one isn't possible without the other? In its wordplay it forgets to be single-minded, remembers unadmitted parts, spins wildly off track, the pithy kiss of kith, that branching embrace of one's friends and neighbouring trees, grass, cats offering alternate relations. Such writing, you see as you read it, refuses the "normal" constraints of English, refuses the lines of the usual anthropocentric, let alone phallogocentric, let alone familial (that old familiar) script.

The In-Between is Reciprocal

Reading the writing a woman writes as she reads out her life, a woman reader will often find herself reading in her own life there between the lines. This in-between space is not merely empty space between two definitive lines of print. It is also the space of what is indefinite, intermingled, shared, like the air we share with trees. In this oxygen-carbon dioxide exchange, we experience a reciprocity. The reciprocal then is responsive to the terms of exchange, transforming and returning what is taken in, sustaining a vital polylogue that is shared. Like talk. Like the relations between a feminist writer and her audience—but the old terms won't do. Tree-talk, tree-breath branching out to you, and your breath, each of you, informing, sending back your own addenda, further leaflets in exchange.

In short, the exchange in feminist writing continually transforms and returns women's lives in the articulation of a vision where we meet. A conversation in writing. A writing conversant with itself as writing-in-process and subversive of the already written. Duras again: "You have to disconnect [the text] from its handicap of being part of the written, get it out of this straitjacket of the written, this straitjacket that's regarded as sacred. . . . It has to circulate" (*Woman*, 144). It is this circulation grounded in the oral that characterizes women's culture, books handed on ("you must read this"), stories handed on ("that reminds me of something that happened to a friend"), phrases handed on ("that's what my mother used to say"). A peculiarly shared resonance we have been taught to overlook. But the trivial, we now learn, that which has been rendered invisible, like tree-air we breathe, is key to our own well-being.

I was never more aware of this than when i was writing *Ana Historic,* a fictional autobiography in which whole phrases came back to me that were my mother's, habitual phrases that sounded the very texture of who she is in me and through her the residue of my grandmother— and beyond her, who knows? The long maternal inheritance that shaped me. I discovered that this was not only personal. For when I read from the book women in the audience would laugh with recognition at certain passages, and some of them told me they saw their own mothers in these phrases, these encounters. Evidence of an oral culture in circulation, a culture that has lasted by word of mouth and is now passing into writing. This sense of a larger inheritance which embeds the personal runs counter to the ideology of the self-created individual. Telling it requires a narrative of subtle interrelations, a matrix as significant as the individual figures which flare into focus and then recede into its texture, its textuality even (word by word by word).

Collaboration as Slippage

If writing is itself reciprocal of so much that surrounds it, then collaborative writing is a more intense experience of reciprocity, of mutual exchange between two minds with two distinctive ways of moving in and through language. Here the in-between space the reciprocal works is that between sameness and difference. The apparent sameness of two women writing, even two lovers embracing similar poetics, is immediately undermined by their different personal vocabularies, the different dance of association a single word may call up for each of them. In a sequence of interleafed entries written in a strategy of call and response, Betsy Warland and i wrote "Reading and Writing

Between the Lines," which talks about what collaboration means to each of us even as we're engaged in doing it. Notions of power embedded in the political use of collaboration are sounded in the first entry, which, to counter them, embraces a "working together reciprocally" between already-drawn lines of sameness and difference. In this in-between space we discover pleasure-holes of wordplay that leak meaning.

The second entry responds to this by illustrating meaning-leak in a semantic play with the root of collaboration, "*collabi*, to slip together." Meaning-slippage, seductive by-play, wet labia, "labyl mynde" and labial phonetics all find a place in a joyous slide of meaning in rhythmic lines across the page.

But this is slippery ground, threatening. The individual ego, which wants to control meaning, rears its head in the form of territorial fear, fear of losing singularity of voice or vision, fear of "being taken off in a different direction altogether" ("Reading" 84). In this dance who's leading anyway? The invitation you thought you'd left (to tango, say—it takes two) may be shifted entirely by your collaborator's desire to pirouette (or your own, for that matter). What is fascinating in this process is the way certain words and images get picked up and translated in your partner's alternate context, even deconstructed in unforeseen ways. Always there is "the tension necessary between what gets said and what gets written or left (out in the dark . . ." ("Reading" 86). Authorial intention, that shaping urge, has to give up its control for the writing to play with, truly respond to, what's given. The overriding metaphors for collaboration shift from war zone to seduction to dancing in the dark to playing cards, this "doubling up of the/ chance of language the cards up/ our sleeves" ("Reading" 87). Yet, the dance continues in the very interplay of those individual pronouns *you & i,* which gradually uncovers a collective we, and the sequence finally concludes "when we interwrite/we call each other's u-phonies out of the dark out of the blue out of / the glare of white" (1988, 90)—the white, i might add, of the inadmissible: the falseness of those fronts, those drawn lines of being singular (alone and only) we like to adopt.

Reading between the lines allows us to see connection. And the writing, in order not to kill that radiating connection with single-minded logic, plays with conventional syntax, makes room for telling words to double back, repeat, refract, reconnect in unexpected ways. It leaves gaps for them to resonate through any reader responsive to them.

This resonance is so multiplicit and various that no one reader, no one writer can carry all of it. That is the delight of the in-between. Every story has its versions as each teller leaves the imprint of her particular words, her particular way of relating. Every reader also reads in her own versions, which respond to, are called up by, what she is reading. This one word, *relation,* carries so much of the act of telling, the act of connecting (kin *and* kith) across the conventional gap between writer and audience, a gap which disappears as we approach that point where language leaps, metaphoric transport, and we cohere in the charged energy of connection.

Vancouver. Sep. 23. 88

what i haven't managed to investigate in journal-writing workshops like
the one at Clam Bay Farm is the <u>production</u> of self—think i stopped
keeping a journal because i grew bored with the self the journal-writing
was producing—that self-justified self. what i love about Joanna Field's
book [A Life of One's Own] are her probings behind the assumed self—
contra-indications for alternate ways of reading "me"

~ ~ ~

Sept. 28. 88

<u>Novel</u>: Teresa Stratas singing Weill—something terribly old & familiar in
that sorrow—could have been her music, my mother's—how she was
always listening to an early sorrow in herself—

     —lateral thinking instead of linear—how the various
levels of existence come together or at least get sounded at once—
the quickly changing moods of Weill, the anger & the sorrow, both—&
another sorrow rises out of the lateral recognition that two entirely
different time periods (hers & mine) coincide in the downward fall of a
single melodic phrase—"I'm a Stranger Here Myself" could have been a
3rd epigraph for Vancouver Poems, which i thought my take on a city
that would never seem hers—

     —how long do we go on carrying our mothers' sorrow?

~ ~ ~

Saltspring Aug. 12. 89

Dear Penn*,

It was good to get that letter from you yesterday as you'd been much on my mind. And i'm so sorry to hear about the time you've been having. Oh Penn, we <u>are</u> all getting older, aren't we? I think about that piece you wrote about never imagining you'd have an old age because you always expected the nuclear cataclysm would happen before that, & how it resonated with me. And here we are with our bodies we can no longer rely on. After Betsy & i moved to the island in mid-May i more or less collapsed —couldn't work for more than an hour without feeling absolutely exhausted & having to lie down wherever i was. We had everything to unpack, a huge garden to plant, our several writing/editing projects to accomplish, & i just couldn't, didn't have it. Doctors thought it was mono but now say it was adrenal gland fatigue.

Anyway i'm feeling more like my old self, the garden in full bloom (masses of nasturtiums around the vegetables, you should see it) & we're almost totally unpacked (only 5 boxes of books to go). Kit is going to a state college just outside of Olympia to take their film & video program, & i'm glad he's figured out what he wants to do.

As we work quietly together in the garden, Bet & i, there are many hours to think in between the hands weeding or picking beans or berries. I think about bp [Nichol] & now Bronwen [Wallace], & Ken Adachi, so close together—& Gwen MacEwen before that. Death in all this abundance. Present like an undertone, like the past & its underlay. I love living on an island again (even though it's so climatically different, but the views of sun glinting off the sea between other islands reminds me of Penang) & we both love living beside this green lake with its changing moods.

<u>Later:</u> just blanched & froze 13 lbs. of green beans. Working with Betsy & [her brother] Steven in the kitchen, sun pouring in the window off the lake, getting into the rhythms of collective work—reminded me of the hours canning Okanagan peaches & apricots with my mother, her delight & pride in seeing rows & rows of stored summer gold glinting in the dark of the

* Penn Kemp

basement wardrobe for winter—pride at accomplishing something she never dreamed she would or could do in Penang days. Feel some of that here too. But we'll have to find a balance between desk work & garden work—after all we moved for more writing time. Next year will be a smaller garden i hope....

So, Penn, like you i haven't done much writing lately. The next novel eats away at the back of my mind, not unpleasantly, just a small ghost nibbling away at my sleep.

~ ~ ~

Self-Representation and Fictionalysis

Written initially for a Women's Studies conference, "Gender and the Construction of Knowledge," at the University of British Columbia in September 1989, this essay was later published in Tessera 8 *(1990) and in a collection of papers from that conference,* Anatomy of Gender: Women's Struggle for the Body, *edited by Valerie Raoul and Dawn Currie. The word-play with* whole *(w + hole) owes something to Gail Scott's deconstruction in "Shaping a Vehicle for Her Use" (1989 version), although we each read our deconstruction differently.*

For the critic, the question behind autobiography seems to be how the writer represents herself. For the writer it is how she represents others. An interesting differential which, in either case, brings up the notion of truth and how or whether it differs from fiction. The writer worries about the difference between how she sees the people she writes about and how they see themselves. The critic looks at the self that is being presented and its difference from what is known about the writer's life, the facts, say. Or "the (f) stop of act," as Annie puts it in *Ana Historic*, isolating fact like the still photo as a moment frozen out of context, that context which goes on shifting, acting, changing after the f-stop has closed its recording eye. The fact a still frame. The self framed she suspects, caught in the ice of representation.

As if there were a self that existed beyond representation as some sort of isolatable entity. And then, for company's sake, your self-representation, your self and your self-representation sitting side by side or, better yet, coinciding. And without that coincidence someone will say, "Oh, she's making herself out to be . . ." Oh dear, fiction as falsity.

Fiction, however, has always included the notion of making, even making something up (as if that something had never existed before), and goes back to a very concrete Indo-European word, *dheigh,* meaning to knead clay. In many creation myths, a goddess or a god molded us and made us, touched us into life, made us up. Out of nothing, out of whole cloth as the saying goes. And so, this nothing-something, or this-something-that-is-also-nothing, insists, as a species, on hanging desperately onto its Somethingness.

Fact or photo or figure (even clay), separate from ground, but not ground, not that . . . facelessness. Women are ground, women are nature. . . . Well, we've heard all that, and for us it's no small feat to be Something, given the ways our culture reinforces the notion that we are less Something than men. And yet we continually demonstrate our abilities to generate something out of almost nothing: a whole baby, a whole book, the whole cloth of a life.

To pick up that phrase "out of whole cloth" is to find an odd reversal, given that "whole" means healthy, undivided, intact, the whole of something. How is it that the whole phrase has come to mean pure fabrication, a tissue of lies?

Whole the other side of hole, w (for women?) the transforming link. We can't seem to avoid the notion that making and the thing made— tissue, or text for that matter, since they come from the same root —have, at root, nothing: "you made it up," or more usually, "you just made it up" (as if making were easy). In our culture of ready-mades, making anything is an accomplishment, making something of yourself even more so, but add that little word "up" and you add speciousness, you add a sneer. Children learn that dressing them-selves is an achievement, but dressing up is only play, child's play as we say of something easy. Yet as children we know that play is not only easy, it is also absorbing and immensely serious, that play is the actual practice (not factual but *act*-ual) of who else we might be.

A powerful put-down that word "up." Does it imply we're trying to imi-tate the gods and have no business reaching a notch higher on the scale of creation, especially when it comes to creating ourselves? Or is that scale fictional too and "up" merely indicates we're getting close to something nonhierarchical but just as significant as in "i'm waking up"?

Perhaps what we wake up to in autobiography is a beginning realiza-tion of the whole cloth of ourselves in connection with so many others. Particularly as women analyzing our lives, putting the pieces together, the repressed, suppressed, putting our finger on the power dynamics at play. It is exactly in the confluence of fiction (the self or selves we might be) and analysis (of the roles we have found ourselves in, defined in a complex socio-familial weave), it is in the confluence of these two that autobiography occurs, the writing self writing its way to life, whole life. This is the practice of the imaginary in its largest sense, for without vision we can't see where we're going or even where we are. Autobiography is not separable from poetry for me on this ground i would call fictionalysis: a self-analysis that plays fictively with the primary images of one's life, a fiction that uncovers analytically that territory where fact and fiction coincide.

In *Ana Historic*, Annie and Ina discuss the difference between story and history, between making things up (out of nothing) and the facts, those frozen somethings of evidence. But what is evident to Annie is not always evident to Ina, because in each of them the seeing occurs in differently informed ways. Clearly, there are different kinds of seeing. For Annie the facts are "skeletal bones of a suppressed body the story is," and that suppressed body which can be ressurected by dint of making up is the unwritten story of who (else) each of the women in the book might be. It is through analysis, analysis of the social context each of them inhabits, that Annie can write her way through the bare bones of who they apparently are to the full sense and the full sensory body of who each of them might be, if they could imagine to their fullest their other i's, their real-(other)-i-zations.

And why isn't the imaginary part of one's life story? Every poet knows it is, just as i know that in inventing a life for Mrs. Richards, i as Annie (and Annie isn't me though she may be one of the selves i could be) invented a historical leak, a hole in the sieve of fact that let the shadow of a possibility leak through into full-blown life. History is not the dead and gone; it lives on in us in the way it shapes our thought and especially our thought about what is possible. Mrs. Richards is a historical leak for the possibility of lesbian life in Victorian British Columbia, which like some deep-packed bedrock continues to underlie the leather shops and tinted glass of our high-rise 1990s. We live in that context: the actuality of both. Just as we also live in the context of salmon rivers polluted with dioxins, harassed abortion clinics, Hong Kong's historic jitters, half-hidden memories of child abuse and whatever hungry ghosts still pursue each one of us—to pull only a few threads of the whole cloth. The context is huge, a living tissue we live together with/in.

To write a whole autobiography, i mean autobiography in its largest sense of self writing life, not the life of a unified self but the life a writing self writes its way to, is to reach for what is almost unwriteable, a hole in that other sense. Yet autobiography until recently was set aside as a minor form, a sort of documentary support, like letters or journal writing, for the great texts. Its significance lay in its veracity, the faithfulness with which it followed the lifeline, the overall narrative of its writer's life, without leaving any holes or gaps, certainly without contradiction. The lifeline after all was supposed to represent a single line, just as the writer's representation of herself was supposed to be a true likeness—like what? Given the whole cloth, the truth of ourselves is so large it is almost impossible to write. It is full of holes, pulled threads (multiple lines), figures indistinct from ground.

Here we run up against the reductiveness of language which wants to separate truth from fiction, figure from ground, self from nothing. Who's the creator here anyway? Maybe language after all, despite itself. But that's only if we can subvert its mainline story, that black stands to white as woman to man, that is, for the sake of definition (which language is all about) as ground to figure. Language defines Something, the subject let's say, as different from any thing and any other who is merely undifferentiated object. We begin to see the bias of the subject operating here and that this subject who so dominates the stage of representation is white, heterosexual, middle class, monological, probably Christian and usually male. Wherever we as women overlap with any of those aspects we inherit that bias. It leaks out everywhere in the most familiar of colloquial phrases, of idiomatic usage, in the very words that fall out of our mouths. Yet these are the words we have—and only by varying them (disrespectfully the subject might say, intent on the singular line of his story), only by altering them infinitesimally, undermining what they say, bending them into knots, into not's and un-'s, can we break the rigid difference between figure and ground which preserves that figure's hegemony, his "truth." No wonder women have such difficulty with the truth—such a single-minded, simple-minded truth it is, with no sense at all of the truth of the ground, of that which bears us in all our harrowing complexity: context.

Autobiography has come to be called life-writing which i take to mean writing for your life, and as such it suggests the way in which the many small real-(other)-i-zations can bring the unwritten, unrecognized, ahistoric ground of a life into being as a recognizable power or agency. This happens when we put together the disparate parts of our lives and begin to see the extensiveness of that cloth of connectedness we are woven into. Then we begin, paradoxically, to weave for ourselves the cloth of our life as we want it to be. For it is in the energetic imagining of all that we are that we can enact ourselves. Every woman we have read who has written about women's lives lives on in us, in what we know of our own capacity for life, and becomes part of the context for our own writing, our own imagining.

When text becomes context, when it leaves behind the single-minded project of following a singular lifeline, a singular i, when it drops out of narrative as heroic climax and opts for narrative as the relation of context, of what surrounds us, then we are in the presence of a writing for life, a writing that ditches dualistic polarities (the good guys vs. the bad guys, gays, bitches, blacks . . . you see how many of us there are), dodges the hierarchies (the achieved, the significant vs. the inessential, the failed—which goes to the root of our fear about life: was it all for nothing?). It's all there in the so-called "nothing."

Saltspring. Aug. 89

still a sense of what? dismay, recoil, seeing my work from the outside as Lola & Frank read it [*line* 13, spring 1989]—now Audrey's comment in her interview with Eleanor [*Tessera* 5, September 1988] returns—& i had so much trouble at the time with her anti-theory stance—but what returns is her sense of the critic "putting Martian labels" on her writing, which i understand now means representing it in a way that makes it unrecognizable to her.

seeing from the outside/ seeing from the inside: shifts in perspective. i do recognize their right, L.'s & F.'s, to their own perspectives—yes, but how far? what to do with this sense that they misrepresent my work for their own theoretical purposes?

the label that feels most Martian is Lola's "vulvalogocentrism"—which pretends to ignore the long history of the absence of women's subjectivity we're all writing our way through, the negation & inferiorizing of the female body, particularly the erasure of lesbian desire. B. thinks there's an unstated fear behind this label—that writing ourselves IN as lesbians equals taking over ALL sites of representation—why else would L. suggest that A.H. is "prescriptive" in its "erotic choice"?

& of course there's the essentialism rap: that i'm stuck in "the conceptual frame of a universal sex opposition"— applied to what is, among other things, a coming-out novel! L. overlooks the real social context that coming-out occurs in (that gender-opposition frame so deeply engrained it constructs "woman")—& why it can be such a long struggle to own your lesbian desire. not to mention how owning it alters how you see that frame.

something about what's foreground, what's background for each of us— that in the foreground women occupy in the novel, their differences (refracted through Annie's desire) are the pull of connection too. for A. this works across the generational divide—how putting unnoticed fragments together from an earlier woman's life (mere background in the old frame) leads to a shift in perspective that radically alters that same frame she grew up inside, makes it possible for her to see beyond it

okay, so why does it bother me so much? more than Frank's related charge that i'm re-inscribing "predetermined" gender binaries in *Hug* (as if how we think of them can <u>erase</u> their continuing social effects in our lives!).

—if differences among women are crucial, as they are, why should i expect L. to understand my work any better than F.? it's that "our," it's that "we" again, & the false assumptions of unity implicit in a shared poetic, a friendship, a shared politic—feminism which isn't <u>one,</u> i keep learning over & over. as if Telling It, working on the proceedings with Sky & Lee & Betsy doesn't already teach me this at every meeting.

~ ~ ~

The Coach House Press

401 (rear) Huron Street, Toronto, Ontario, Canada   M5S 2G5   (416) 979-2217

Writing & Gender (an anthology of views by Canadian women)

We've all heard about or participated in the lively debate about the relationship of feminism to writing. The editors welcome proposals for an anthology which will explore the range of viewpoints held by Canadian women who write. Here are some questions we posed to one another in first discussing this anthology. They may be of use to you or you may want to discuss other matters.

Do you consider yourself a feminist?

Do you think feminism has had an effect on the writing and publishing climate in Canada? How?

Has feminism had an effect on your writing?

Do you feel you have a specifically 'female' point of view or feminist P.O.V.? How do you feel about writing in which the author takes a viewpoint other than his/her own, e.g, a woman in male voice or vice versa? If you choose to write from a male viewpoint does it change how you write?

Do considerations of race, class, or sexual orientation affect how you write?

Are you familiar with various currents in feminist literary theory? What about the many different feminist political viewpoints, from radical to moderate? Have these things affected the way you write?

Please drop us a short note indicating whether or not you're interested in contributing to this anthology and give a sense of your general focus. You might choose to discuss the writing of a specific work and the choices made during its creation. We are looking to hear from as wide a range of writers as possible. Margaret Atwood, June Callwood and Phyllis Webb have already committed themselves to writing something.

Please let us know by February 1st, l989 whether or not you'd like to contribute. The Coach House Press has scheduled this book for publication in 1989.

Libby Scheier, Sarah Sheard, Eleanor Wachtel,
editors

Difference (em)bracing

To extend debate about the impact of feminist theory on women's writing in Canada, Libby Scheier, Sarah Sheard and Eleanor Wachtel put out a call for contributions to an anthology which subsequently appeared from Coach House Press in 1990, Language In Her Eye: Views on Writing and Gender by Canadian Women Writing in English. *Trying to combine feminist statement and personal history with free-play in the shifting perspectives of first-, second- and third-person pronouns—and for an audience that wasn't necessarily feminist—my essay resorted to imagistic shorthand that often obscured instead of clarifying. What follows is an attempt to open up that shorthand.*

In not the same person

What is it that makes some words essential, relevant to one woman writer and irrelevant to another? And can we communicate then? What is communication but a sharing of our visions of what is essential? And by that i don't mean to refer to essence but to necessity, that which motivates us as writers. Sometimes in reading as in writing the sudden shift from inessential to essential occurs in the same person (and is she, are you then the same?)—that shift where a word that was merely a concept, existing somewhere out there as an object in flight in the world you read or listen in on (you peripheral to it), and then in a flash this word wings in to the core of your being and you recognize all that it stands for and that you have a stake in it, a share as speaker/writer/reader/listener, all of you there in that active complex, involved in your own assertion of what is meaningful to you.

The difference writing makes when, caught in the act so to speak, you ask yourself questions and discover the words you can stand by are words that stand that ground you have a share in. Feminist, for instance, writing subject, lesbian—words you recognize and have a stake in. Or do you? Ah, this list feels stacked, you think, against you-particular, you-reader, you who suddenly feel excluded by its terms. I, my other choice, also excludes you, except by identification. Public words, words in debate and personal pronouns prove tricky when set side by side. How to set up currents of meaning that ripple out from this you i also am (not third person, as in totally other, and not quite the same as me) to include you as another, an equal centrality equivalent to my own. Transform the metaphor: *you* as a light beam of possibility so large it embraces both of us without setting you in the third person there apart from me. Third person: at a remove. Because we speak about "her" in the third person, "she" is where exclusion takes place. "Feminist," "lesbian" take on other meanings then—they suddenly limit, objectify. But in the first or second person i see who you are, feminist, lesbian: your historicity, your meaning-potential is what i grow into.

So i come to recognize certain words that constitute my body (not exclusive of the psychic terrain my historical body stands for, living tissue embodied memory)—the body of my writing. "Getting to know you" words out there—maybe as other as the King of Siam—written from a white colonial point of view. Those dated words which excited my fifteen-year-old imagination under cloudy skies backlit by the foots and spots of Theatre Under the Stars in Stanley Park, still run through my forty-seven-year-old mind. But now i suspect a hidden imperialism in them: making the other the same and therefore plausible, i.e., plausibly me. This script lies at the heart of fiction and is not what i'm trying to get at, which is the plausible implausibility of living difference as both other and not-other. Other me besides me.

As Virginia Woolf has written of "the sixty or seventy different times which beat simultaneously in every normal human system" (191) and how rarely we manage to synchronize them, or again of "the perfect rag-bag of odds and ends within us—a piece of a policeman's trousers lying cheek by jowl with Queen Alexandra's wedding veil" (49) (this distinctly English and period cultural rag-bag). Or as Hélène Cixous has written of writing as "precisely working (in) the in-between, inspecting the process of the same and of the other without which nothing can live, undoing the work of death—to admit this is first to want the two, as well as both, the ensemble of the one and the other" (254). Women keep trying to write it, what we sense that language resists, structured as it is on the basis of difference as absolute, difference which cannot bear the integration of both/and vision (Rachel Blau DuPlessis 6–7).

It is poetry which pushes the limits of this system, speaks in corresponding differences (differences which speak to each other). Not the same as "same difference," that childhood taunt of dismissal which collapsed difference into an identical same. How to find the words that will stand the corresponding differences of this complexity we glimpse ourselves living, despite the monocultural stereotypes that delude us into thinking difference means an opposition, the utterly singular on one side of a great divide.

Difference is where the words turn depending on who reads them and how we bring who we are to that reading. When we each bring our differences into that reading, the multiple nature of the real begins to be heard.

Arriving at Shared Ground Through Difference

It wasn't sharing but difference in a multiplicity of ways i felt first as a child in Malaya where i was taught the King's (it was then) English, to mind my P's & Q's, to behave and speak "properly," when all the while i was surrounded by other languages that were not proper at all for a white colonial child, but which nevertheless i longed to understand, filled as they were with laughter, jokes, calls, exclamations, comfort, humming. Sometimes rocked to sleep, sometimes teased or scolded, sometimes ignored by the sounds of Cantonese, Malay, Thai, i stood on the fringe and longed to know what the stories were that produced such laughter, such shakings of the head. When my Amahs spoke only English to me, they knew and i knew the monolingual meant no time for play, meant we had to be "proper." O the complexities of the power dynamic between colonial children and their mother-substitutes, these women who had given up the possibility of families for themselves but who nevertheless led other lives, barely heard between the lines proper to their servant roles, and who illicitly imparted some of their culture, some of their life experience to the Mem's children. I grew up loving the emotive sound of women's voices and distrustful of a system that dismissed women's experience in general, and some women's more than others', depending on the colour of their skin and the language(s) they spoke—and many spoke more than the single-minded ruling one.

That the ruling one: my father's talk, fraught with finance and politics, the black and white of communism and democracy, empire and independence, God and flawed humanity. Impromptu history lessons of Sunday afternoons when i watched him clean the family shoes lined up in our 1950s Canadian basement. Yet he told stories too, raconteur in another, nonauthoritative voice, traces of his Malayan days studding his language: *barang, sampan, chichak,* irreplaceable words called up by particular stories retold each time with the zest of original pleasure.

Then there was my mother's tongue: English English with its many intensifiers, its emphatic sentence pitches, its ringing tones of boarding school elocution lessons. Learning to speak properly—"Don't drawl like that."

The trouble was i had become embarrassed by the language i spoke which branded me as both excessive (those intensifiers) and excessively polite in Canadian school yards. My speech sounded exaggerated: "Wha'd ya mean 'awfully sorry'? You're not awful are you?" Sounded pretentious: "Listen, nobody walks on the GRAWSS." At first "wanna," and "movies" and "you guys" sounded funny in my mouth, as if i were trying to speak counterfeit words. But imitation cut both ways: there was now a whole new level of my own vocabulary, words that rang false on the street: cinema, rubbish, being sent to Coventry, not to mention that give-away, Mummy, a world away from Mom. And so i engaged in long battles with her, each of us trying to correct the other, she correcting for purity of origin, while i corrected for common usage—each of us with different versions of the real thing.

By the time i entered UBC in 1960, Canadian was something i had mastered—and i use that word deliberately. As a student of literature, almost all my literary models, quite literally "the masters" of English (or American—at that time we didn't study Canadian) literature, were men. As a young writer, the contemporary poetry other writers pointed me to was largely written by men. My own "masters" (in that sense of mentors) were Charles Olson, Robert Duncan, Robert Creeley and their masters, William Carlos Williams, Ezra Pound, Louis Zukofsky. Somehow reading "the poet, he" to include me, i trained myself in that poetic, the injunctions to get rid of the lyric ego, not to "sprawl" in loose description or emotion ungrounded in image, to pay strict attention to the conjoined movement of body (breath) and mind in the movement of the line, though it didn't occur to me then to wonder whether my somewhat battered female ego was anything like a man's or whether my woman's body had different rhythms from his or whether my female experience might not give me an alternate "stance" in the world (one that wasn't so much "in" as both in & outside of a male-dominated politic & economy). But there were cracks, fissures that led me to another writing world. Through Robert Duncan's prose poems & Charles Olson's essays, i remembered my original delight in the extendible and finely balanced nature of the sentence ungoverned by line breaks (a different sort of sprawl). Duncan led me to Gertrude Stein and her play with emphasis, with difference in repetition, with the passionate nature of the loopy speaking sentence, peculiarly a woman's in her work. Duncan led me to H.D. too, another sort of passion, the passion of vision, of interwoven imageries lifted live from a wealth of spiritual traditions and fused, reclaimed in light of her lived experience, the H.D. of long poems and the H.D. of novels documenting the struggle of a woman to live her particular intersection of past and present.

Impossible to list here all the reading paths (as divergent as Anais Nin, Maxine Hong Kingston, Phyllis Webb, Marguerite Duras, Zora Neale Hurston, Nicole Brossard) which led me to the hidden and astonishingly varied tradition of women's writing—the other side of that man-in-the-moon face polished and presented to us as the shining side of "Contemporary Literature" when i was in school. The dark side, a wonderful colloquy of women's voices writing about the "trivial," the taboo and tacit: solitude verging on madness, women's social roles and loss of self, excessive passion, a whole female erotic, daily doubts that give the lie to philosophic certainties, companionship with animals and trees, women's companionship despite double standards in (and within) sex and race, double standards everywhere and women speaking of and writing on that double edge, in touch with one another's difficult balance there. And that was the excitement, the lifting of a horizon, that here was an ongoing dialogue where women were central, not marginal, where women were delighting in writing the complex i (fem.), not trying to write like "the poet, he" in all his singular authority.

The Singularly Complex

This dialogue that our writing enters is a singularly (as in deviating from the norm) complex one because it includes, it must include, voices from so many fringes, not just that fringe, women (translated as white, middle class, heterosexual, Anglo-Canadian) that has been gradually getting so legitimated it would seem to be moving into centre. Becoming aware of dialogue on the (many) fringes, listening to other women's words, realities, is to engage in a delicate balance between recognition of difference and recognition of shared ground. The balance between i and we—and neither capitalized nor capitalizing on the other.

To begin with, to write I, to assume my own centrality as ground, goes against the historic burden of gender conditioning and is a frightening first step in autobiography and journal writing. An act of self-assertion. But to write I with some attention is to discover that this singular column with its pedestal and cap, this authorized capital letter vested in the law, far from being monolithically singular is full of holes a wind blows through, whispering contradictory images, rehearsing and resisting others' definitions, feeling sometimes most at home in silence. I, voiced and assertive I, am not always identical with myself, or i am "myself" a multiplicity of presence and absence in different perspectives struggling to speak through rigid assumptions of sameness and identity in the language we have inherited.

Lower-case i becomes a kind of shorthand, then, for this complex of already defined and indefinite (wordless, sometimes) identities. And we? We asserts connection, group identity, solidarity. With it comes an urge to include/exclude. And also an urge to resist being reduced—as Joy Kogawa puts it, "An identity can be a hair coat" (*Telling It*, 123). Because a sense of the actual overlapping boundaries of identities can feel uneasily shifting, nebulous, groups build fences to defend their territory. But just as this i-fraught-with-inner-differences tries to stabilize herself, defend her comfort zone with a monolithic I, so *we* can too easily blur differences between the i's which compose it. A recognition of real disparities in life experience and perceived identity, in privilege and difference from the dominant "norm" is essential here.

There are many we's which any i might feel included in, just as there are many we's which any i might feel excluded from, race, class and sexual orientation being the broadest of distinctions/groupings. Yet each i stands amidst different belongings, inhabits variously contested borderlands, to borrow and translate Gloria Anzaldua's phrase in *Borderlands/La Frontera*. The complex of these for each one of us is not the same as for any other. This makes the differences in our language crucial as they refract a prismatic sense of who we are. And it calls for readers attentive to the full spectrum of those differences as they are articulated in the work of others.

Saltspring. Oct. 2. 89

been here almost 5 months now & the beauty of this place is still
astonishing, ever-changing—late-night glimpses of the lake, stumbling
up for water, half-asleep & stopped by all that glimmering through the
window, huge presence: cottonwoods restless onshore, small waves,
moon track brilliants streaming in—this sense of intimacy, the only one
up to see it—yet not intimate, nothing personal—just standing <u>with</u> it,
coinciding—stumbling around trying to put it into words

       <u>putting</u> into words the problem—to describe something
already there is to *de*-scribe, un-write—since writing's not so much
writing about, around (something out there) but what is happening in the
relations between words as they come up, network their way into being . . .
(a sentence, say)

       yet to write, to activate sensation, set meaning in motion
across skin, the gap between separate bodies reading & writing—that's
the lure. writing itself a metaphor for connectedness in its very language,
that kinetically associative net that registers our being however
momentarily—traces of passage, word-prints for another curious set
of eyes to puzzle through . . . the possibility of connection then

       later:

but words also function to exclude in order to define—*postmodernism* &
feminism, their relations "épineuse" or thorny as Raija Koski so accurately
says in her letter on "Le Discours féminin dans la litt. postmoderne du
Québec." heartening to see the word *postmodern* feminized in relation
to literature. & difficult to verbalize the Anglo part of "le contexte
spécifiquement canadien"—it's so clear that for Quebec, Anglo-Can.
feminist writing doesn't exist: "Les deux mouvements, le féminisme et le
postmodernisme, étaient spécifiquement québécois, quoiqu'ouverts sur
ce qui se passait en France et aux États-unis."

so, it's <u>one-way</u> influence, French to English, for those of us excited by what's been going on in Quebec—an influence experienced here in the West as only a strange marginalization: Sharon Thesen & Diana Hartog see us as merely imitative, Brossardian "cookie-cutters" in the Connie Rooke interview—as if Nicole were the only influence & postmodern feminism can't exist outside of Quebec. let alone the States & all that vital writing in HOW(ever), etc.: still relishing Rachel Blau DuPlessis' clarity in the quote re-found yesterday in my notes from the San Francisco conference [Women Working in Literature II, 1985]: "Syntax in poetry is like narrative in novels—the place where ideology and values are found"

ok, so this intersection Betsy & i & others occupy is a peculiar one: as far as Can. postmodern critics go i'm not postmodern enough, gone lesbian-feminist = gone reductive, fallen into the slough of, not "despond" (i'm climbing out!) but, essentialism. upshot of talk with B. about this panel: to contribute something particular i have to speak from where i stand. "l'écriture au féminine spécifiquement québécoise" has rippled out to the ends of this particular continent of women (writers), but on our coast it alters, grows more literal, more autobiographical as it meets resistance. history meeting utopia? i still believe in the need for utopia, that horizon line we work toward. but if we can't see where we're coming <u>from</u>, how see where we're going? (to reframe a recurring question!)

~ ~ ~

le
discours
féminin
dans la
littérature
post-
moderne
du
québec

The UNIVERSITY *of* WESTERN ONTARIO

Department of French • University College
London, Canada • N6A 3K7

Du 2 au 5 novembre 1989 —

Dans le cadre de ce colloque nous
proposons d'examiner la voix des
femmes dans les textes poétiques,
romanesques et/ou théâtraux
d'écrivaines au Québec au cours des
vingt dernières années.

— avec la participation de:

Louky Bersianik
Nicole Brossard
Robin Edwards Davies
Jo-Anne Elder
Louise Forsyth
Barbara Godard
Maroussia Hajdukowski-Ahmed
Kathleen Kells
Michael Klementowicz
Raija Koski
Susanne de Lotbinière-Harwood
Jeannette Laillou Savona
Jean Levasseur
Daphne Marlatt
Bénédicte Mauguière
Madeleine Ouellette-Michalska
Anne-Marie Picard
Valerie Raoul
Lucie Robert
Lori Saint-Martin
Patricia Smart
France Théoret
Marie Vautier
Christl Verduyn
Maïr Verthuy

JEUDI, LE 2 NOVEMBRE
Séance d'ouverture
Great Hall, Huron College

La Postmodernité

19h.00   Accueil et inscription

20h.00   Ouverture du colloque
Minnette Gaudet, Doyenne
associée (UWO)
Raija Koski (UWO)

Conférence inaugurale
Janet Paterson (Toronto)
*"Postmodernisme et féminisme:
où sont les jonctions?"*

Réception

VENDREDI, LE 3 NOVEMBRE
Première Séance
McKellar Room, UCC 251

Présidée par **Marilyn Kidd**
Huron College, UWO

Théorie et discours: richesse et diversité de perspectives

9h.00   **Barbara Godard** (York)
"Frictions"

9h.45   **Maïr Verthuy** (Concordia)
*"Du centre à la marge: pour une
écoute des voix autres (immigrées,
femmes des minorités visibles, etc.)
dans la littérature féminine au Québec"*

10h.30   Pause

10h.45   **Maroussia Hajdukowski-Ahmed**
(McMaster)
*"Le discours féminin post-
moderne: une contradiction dans
les termes"*

11h.30   **Madeleine Ouellette-Michalska**
*"L'effacement de la mère et
le deuil des possibles"*

12h.15   Déjeuner

Re-Belle at the Writing Table

At a conference on Québécoise writing at the University of Western Ontario in 1989, i spoke on a writers' panel titled "Femmes rebelles devant la table d'écriture" with Louky Bersianik, Nicole Brossard, Susanne de Lotbinière-Harwood, Madeleine Ouellette-Michalska and France Théoret. This talk was subsequently included in a proceedings with the conference title, Le discours féminin dans la littérature postmoderne du québéc, edited by Raija Koski, Kathleen Kells and Louise Forsyth (1993). What follows is an edited version.

Conventionally, a rebel (moving from French to English, the noun dropped its feminine "elle" to stand in solitary masculine splendour, "el" masquerading as universal) has been defined as one who refuses allegiance to an established government, party, law. To be a rebel turns on the issue of allegiance. Yet rebels are not without their own brand of allegiance to something that stands outside the established, the orthodox. This question of allegiance (its feudal associations) or loyalty (those patriotic undertones) or even comradeship (definitely a socialist echo) . . . these terms, so heavily freighted with a patriarchal history of use, seem to have no immediate cognates in the feminine. To recontextualize, then, in a different system of values: to posit a sense of connectedness. And translate it into the scene of writing with a question: for whom, with whom do i feel myself writing? This question has been crucial in my evolution as a writer.

In her paper, "Re-belles et infidèles," Susanne de Lotbinière-Harwood spins a new turn on the conventional phrase, "belles infidèles," for translations that "deliberately distort or appropriate the source-language work to suit the translator's political or cultural agenda" (98). By adding that little prefix "re-" to "belles" she gives us rebels in the feminine and a term for her own subversive practice of feminist translation which "foreground[s] the issue of gender" (101). Demonstrating how words cannot be taken at *face* value, she retrieves "rebel" for women's use, refocussing its revolutionary value by distorting the established criterion for female representation ("belle," beauty) within the symbolic order. "Re-belle" suggests, through its emphasis on "re-," re-drawing the terms by which we see ourselves, and further, re-drawing them in light of our connection with one another. I've left "fidèle" or allegiance behind, but it comes up here in this connectedness.

When I began writing, i began, as i suppose most young writers do, by writing alone, not knowing that what i sensed was shared by others. I encountered the scene that would generate my first allegiance in 1960 when i went to the University of British Columbia and met a very active group of writers, mostly male. I began going to regular meetings of this group, getting embroiled in debates over poetics, submitting my work for criticism and publication in their magazines. I was one of the youngest writers in that group and consequently many of the older students were mentors for me. Yet because i was a woman, i was never sure whether i was really a validated *writing* member. I wanted to be taken seriously as a poet (o that passive voice!) but was taken more seriously as a woman, the object of a few love poems, one or two about my deficiencies as a "beauty"—"belle" in its conventional sense. Yet rebel in its universal (masculine) form was a role i identified with, not really knowing why, supposing that it was because this was an embattled group of writers much criticized for adapting an American postmodern poetics to a Canadian West Coast locale and for writing critically about the closed forms of much establishment poetry. The group saw itself as postmodernist, involved in a writing that was processual, nonlinear, open-ended, and intent on decentering the Western human subject (that universal again, but i didn't at that point have a gender critique for it). And all this while, in Quebec, *la modernité* never stopped evolving into what we would call postmodernist forms, and then, with fiction-theory, a distinctly feminist version of postmodernism.

I want to make a point of this bit of history because English-Canadian feminist writing is often characterized by francophone critics as irrevocably tied to realism and unacquainted with postmodernist techniques. Yet there are a number of postmodern feminist writers west of Quebec—Lola Lemire Tostevin, Smaro Kamboureli, Judith Fitzgerald, Penn Kemp to name a few—who served their apprenticeship, as i did, with largely male postmodernist groups and who then moved on to evolve a feminist perspective.

Feminist critical theory has subsequently amassed pages on why women find hybrid forms, nonlinear structures, and a processual and fragmentary approach most adaptable to our sense of the real (and this includes our imaginary). It wasn't till i started reading feminist theory that i understood why these structures and techniques were so adaptable to what i have to say as a woman and as a lesbian writer. Coincident with this awareness came an extraordinarily vivid sense of audience.

As i read my work to live audiences, an almost tactile sense of an audience being "with" the work began to make itself apparent. Then as women came up to me after a reading to express their excitement at having heard verbalized some perception that confirmed their own, that elicited some making-sense of their own experience, i became aware of an unspeakable beauty in women. Not just the unspeakable beauty of bodies that don't conform to standard sexist notions of female beauty, not just the unacknowledged strength of women freed from the confines of "feminine" behaviour, but the beauty of coming into words, words that struggle to convey what language cannot, without subversion, confirm: the affirmation of our embodied and multiphasic being *from where we stand*, astride so many versions of difference. From this standpoint, in resistance to so much ready-made definition on all sides, everything has to be worded differently so as not to comply, not to be complicit with that repression. A repression which can also be found, and devastatingly so, inside ourselves. That is the beauty and the terror of the place from which we speak.

As i began to recognize this beauty, so i began to desire evidence of it in our collective body. Not to have, or to own, but to experience it in circulation among us, in communication between us. In short, i understood that first of all i write for and with women who share this excitement of coming in(to) language as we come to a different sense of being.

Perhaps what i'm trying to articulate here is a theory of emerging interrelatedness in lesbian writing, but i know that it also embraces women who are not lesbian, as the result, it may be, of what Luce Irigaray calls our "plural" sexuality. I know that it also embraces our connectedness to what surrounds us, the matter, the matrix of our shared lives, our ecosphere, the multidimensional "ground" we stand on and with. I've always thought that writing has to do with embodiment in all senses, and by that i also mean the very delicate crossing of the thresholds of separate bodies.

Getting a sense of this generative communication with an audience behind or beyond the literal of words, a certain *rapport d'addresse*, the term Nicole Brossard brought into discussion one summer afternoon in Vancouver several years ago, has meant a different kind of focus in my writing. Coming to know my companions in this project, our conversations across time and place, books and ideas exchanged, all this focusses the difference that "re-belle" embodies.

The writers at this table represent for me a continuously opening terrain of writing, even in our differences of language and culture. And the value of this evolving matrix of thought/ writing/ discussion can never be underestimated. Louky Bersianik speaks of Virginia Woolf as her literary mother: it seems to me that as women writing now, our work goes on mothering each other in generative circuits, both within French and within English as two distinct cultures waving to each other across the language divide, and as common ground differently arrived at.

This sense of our collective work mothering each of us—mothering new work too, but i want to focus here on the evolution of our individual psyches in response to shared dialogue—this sense of the permeability of that conventional divide between writing and living, between fiction and reality, is difficult for some postmodernist critics of feminist writing to come to terms with. Our writing is real to us in the way it changes our lives: changing the language, subverting its patriarchal value-freight, puts us in a new relationship to all that surrounds us and gains us new versions of ourselves, of what is possible. As Linda Hutcheon points out, feminism or feminisms, as she wisely pluralizes, work for change whereas postmodernism remains finally complicit with the cultural structures it critiques (43).

The difference lies not just in allegiance to an ideology but in something i can only articulate as this writing for-whom/ with-whom that allows us to see the unspeakable beauty of where we connect, a beauty beyond face value.

Saltspring. Aug. 9. 91

Dear Kathy*,

I can't begin to tell you how important Warner & Sandilands' *Women Beyond the Wire* has been/is being. I'm reading it slowly because it's heartbreaking material. Thank you so much for getting it out for me on your card. Each morning when i read a little further, i end up weeping for all their pain, & yet it's also an extraordinary testimonial to the endurance of women, not just plain physical endurance (god knows they were called on enough for that) but spiritual, for want of a word to name that profound ability many women have to make even the worst of situations liveable, bearable. Even when they were slowly starving to death, with all the diseases malnutrition brings—beri-beri, dysentery & typhoid from appallingly bad sanitation, malaria & dengue fever—they celebrated each other's birthdays, wrote poems for each other, drew sketches of the camps, remembered songs & formed an "orchestra" of voices which actually could perform Ravel's "Bolero" by memory.

I don't really know how it compares to the Jewish experience in the German concentration camps, though the details of their last transport by boat & rail, especially the rail part, to a camp in the mountains of southern Sumatra are similar to reports of the transport of Jewish people. Utterly unbearable trip for 3 days, very little food or water & many of the women already dying or very ill.

The extraordinary thing is that some part of me recognizes these experiences, already knows it, i don't understand how. Was it so much in the air when i was a small child? When they discovered at the end of the war how awful conditions were in those Japanese camps. I don't remember anyone talking about it—no one speaks of it now, except for a handful of books, mostly by survivors. Yet this is an extraordinary part of women's history: what women learned about themselves under these conditions, how they came to see the society they had been taken from, what they managed to change in the way they constructed a new society within the camps.

* Kathy Mezei

I think about these things—what women learned they would do for other women & children, the inner resources they discovered, the strength they could draw on from their strongest friendships & a sense of community —this despite the short tempers, constant anxiety, daily irritations with each other, & awful illness. One survivor told the editors: "For all the hardships, without families and all the pressures of the real world bearing down, there was time to think, to work out what kind of person you really were, to indulge in off-beat or eccentric behaviour that would have been impossible in conventional surroundings. I found myself there."

How much of this will find its way into the novel is difficult to see right now. I struggled with the notion that i had no right to write out of the excessive pain of these experiences because i hadn't experienced them. But then decided that i could address them, the women of these camps, in the second person. It's easiest for me to imagine writing to one of the young girls who saw so much that their social conditioning had in no way prepared them for, who would have been curious & open in a way some of the older women couldn't have been. But i'm writing to different women of differing ages through the all-encompassing "you" which is sometimes singular & sometimes plural. And i feel called upon to write it, somehow, in memory of the women whose graves are lost now in the jungle. Does this sound terribly presumptuous? I remember your reaction to Yolande Villemaire's novel about the Jewish concentration-camp experience. But i do feel close to this because these were people of my parents' generation & way of life, some of them would have been acquaintances or friends. How we elide painful experience—i wish they were alive so i could ask. They hardly ever spoke of it & all i know is that my godfather was one of those who died building the infamous Burma Railway the Japanese made half-starved POWs from Changi (the Singapore camp) construct through the jungle.

If we could have coffee together in the Granville Market we could talk about all this, but failing that, this letter. You'll be coming back from Hornby Island in the next day or so (hope you had some good weather up there, it hasn't been great here the last few days) & i'm determined to write you a letter you can take with you to France so that, once settled, you can pull it out & write me back.

So here's a copy of Sharon Thesen's article & maybe we can continue the discussion we began on the phone the other day about how we feel about theory these days. Sharon goes so far in the anti-theory direction that i have no sympathy with her position: to call all theory totalitarian is to dismiss it in a rather total way! There's no sense of how one might choose between theory that's useful, stimulating, opens new avenues of thought, & theory that seems exclusive, "in-house," or "prescriptive" (to use her term)—she lumps together different kinds of theory & tars them all. But for me what's troubling about more & more critical theory is the way its specialized language ends up talking to itself. This has to do with how i feel as a writer, that i can't write (fiction, poetry) out of the language of theory, though i might usefully read it. And it's not entirely true that i can't write out of it, because theory certainly underlies my recent books, even if it's theory translated. And i've certainly been stimulated as a writer by certain theorists—Chodorow, Cixous, Rich, Kristeva, Daly though i know it's unfashionable to mention Daly now that she's been censored with that all-powerful label "essentialist."

Okay, so now we're getting to the heart of the problem, the fashionability of theory, how it's developed camps with rival claims to seeing through each other's blind spots, & how writers get dumped for not being rigorous enough instead of being appreciated for the territory they <u>have</u> opened up. It's unfashionable, for instance, to even talk about "women's experience" —that's essentialist, it implies an irreduceability, no recognition of the way we're socially constructed, & variably so. But i know i write out of experience, & what <u>moves</u> me as a writer isn't initially or even primarily theoretical, though theory often helps me understand it.

Do write & tell me how you see your relationship to theory, both as a critic & as a writer—what your difficulties are & whether any of what i've said here touches on what you feel about it. If you don't have a copy of the *Open Letter* issue with Smaro's [Kamboureli] article, the one Sharon's reacting to, let me know & i'll send it.

I'll miss you while you're gone. But who knows, maybe letters will take us even further than occasional snatched coffees in our exchange of ideas (& experiences!)

~ ~ ~

Saltspring. February ? 92

[Marianne] Hirsch writing on Christa Wolf's extraordinary *Patterns of Childhood*—which she calls, it seems right, "a group autobiography, the autobiography of a generation who lived its 'model' or 'monstrous' childhood during W.W. II in Germany"—points to the narrative question linking all 3 time-strata in the novel: "how did we become as we are today?" maybe it's the key question behind any autobiographical writing, especially if the past is questionable in some way—

& this from CW, the opening lines of her novel:
"What is past is not dead; it is not even past. We cut ourselves off from it; we pretend to be strangers."

how relate to the monstrous in our history?
                    which keeps rearing its bullish head in new forms: the call from Janice [Williamson] last night telling me about going to her univ. office & finding KILL slogans daubed all over her door—the chilling echo, though neither of us mentioned it, of the Montreal massacre—where i wade through fear, she feels outrage

or maybe it's despair: wading through this ruined labyrinth full of water, walls daubed with hostile slogans, no way out—

                    hard to acept that the world as we work for it to be, a just world, isn't that way, isn't ever going to be—Phyllis [Webb] in Smaro's interview with her in *West Coast Line* talks about how hard it was to give up the dream of a just society—yes, & everywhere now the crumbling of the left, a sense of being outnumbered—is giving up dangerous?—Phyllis locates the dream within a patriarchal structure (socialism) but what about the feminist one? maybe what has to be given up is a sense of childish disappointment that things aren't better after all the years of collective work (but they were *supposed* to be!)—abandoning the us vs. them, outnumbered framework—feeling closer to the Buddhist view:

that to recognize we're all drowning in this ocean of suffering doesn't mean giving up on the will to work to release beings from it, does mean recognizing what keeps us locked inside the ruin

this, to hold as a sort of mental compass: CW again from *The Reader & the Writer*: "I have discovered that one must at all costs try to break through and go beyond the circle of what we know, or think we know, about ourselves."

~ ~ ~

Salvaging: The Subversion of Mainstream Culture in Contemporary Feminist Writing

In the fall of 1991 I was asked to speak at the University of New Brunswick and began writing the following essay for the UNB's Women's Studies Department. It was delivered in January 1992 and then again, in revised version, to the Centre for Studies in Gender Relations at UBC in October 1992. It was published in Trivia 20 (1992). *A number of concerns surfaced at the time of writing: a concern, for instance, that correct feminist theory was becoming a divisive force between feminists, as well as a concern that social backlash against feminist visibility was increasing—witness the massacre of women engineering students at the Montreal Polytechnic in 1989.*

Preamble

To write *we* these days is fraught with difficulty, as a decade or more of resistance to being spoken for in the women's movement so aptly demonstrates. How write we in the face of well-deserved suspicion about this pluralized first person masquerading as inclusive while it hides its writer's particular set of allegiances, this notoriously general we which can isolate rather than include.

Yet something in me can't abandon the possibility of we. Or, perhaps, can't abandon the hope that we represents: community, recognized commonality, feminist understanding that reaches across different and isolating experiences of oppression to form the basis of solidarity (yes, that political term), to support positive action on behalf of more than oneself.

So, to the Ambit

Salvaging. Subversion. Feminist writing in Canada. Of the three terms, salvaging seems the most unlikely. What could possibly be considered feminist about salvaging which has all sorts of legalistic associations having to do with saving cargo or ships from marine peril? What we call salvage refers to that which is actually still useable although it has been written off as lost or irretrievably damaged. Salvage yards: auto junk yards, wrecks with parts that can still be used. Drift logs from passing booms and salvage operators, who for decades have rounded them up on the coast to sell as useable timber. Salvage: a frontier word with junk associations. What interests me as a feminist writer is the concept embedded in this word of retrieving value from what has been written off. Finding something valuable in trash.

Trash. What can i, as a woman and a lesbian, salvage of value in the culture i live in and yet stand aslant to, if not pushed at times, by sheer misogynist violence, to its outer edges?

An otherness of vision, a turning around of value. Seeing through the echoes of sexual politics still audible in the words *trash* and *wreckage* and *ruin* when applied to women, telltale traces of the old double standard (Victorian and victorious even in our presumably progressive times)—those phrases we all heard as we grew up; "she's just trash" or "she looks so trashy" or "doesn't she look a wreck" or the more dated notion of moral ruin in "a ruined woman." Even in contemporary usage, when we "trash" each other we engage in an act of destruction, reducing the other woman to no account, writing her off, writing off her perspective, her particular history.

If feminists can so readily do to one another what mainstream culture does to us, it's in part because we still unthinkingly perpetuate the dichotomies this culture instills through its battery of acceptable/ unacceptable value checks that separate us off from one another, all those sexist, class-based and racist checks and crossings out. Breaking the power of these dichotomies calls for acts of salvaging, where we can look squarely at the negative set the dominant culture applies and see through it, turning negative into positive within an alternative system of values. Trash as workable wood, something useful for building.

Feminists writing in both French and English in Canada have been raiding the negative placement of women in popular culture to subvert the meanings of that placement. One of the strategies of these salvaging raids is to show how a close attention to language for its power to damn reverses and releases what is damned into language play that creates a different view. In her story "Mirror, Mirror, Tell Me Who is Fairest of All?" France Théoret probes a girl's fear of ruin as the working metonymy for her future amongst those who keep her body under surveillance and in so doing transforms this fear into cultural critique:

> Ruin of the intelligence. Body ruined just as well. The one doesn't go without the other.
>
> 'I'm kept under close watch and don't see anything,' she says to herself.
>
> The bar maid has only to behave herself well. The young lady from the city is too stylish in her dress of red and black wool. Not to mention her fur collars. The young lady

is the same age as the marriageable girls hereabouts. Marriageable daughter, married woman: from sixteen to eighteen years old, the passage. From the father's house to the husband's where she says willingly that she can't manage to live as orderly as her parents. The next year, she wears her first dress of black or forest green brocade.

The bar maid is marriageable. The regulars are thirsty. She serves them, as her mother says. The rounds begin again, rounds of gestures, mechanics of eighteen, twenty hour days. The tiniest space of the imaginary is threatened. All gestures interrupted, there's no respite until the first arrival speaks. To speak, does she want to? Is it even a possible, correct, sensible question? The hotel is not a church, her mother often says to her.

Obviously, this is a lively place. For the relaxation of the worker! Drivers of trucks or bulldozers, masons, the guys in construction, loggers with a chain saw not forgetting the unemployed and welfare cases. 'It's all good money!' the cashier kept saying.

Mirror behind the bar. The painting by Manet, the decoration aged from having seen eighty, one hundred years pass. The decline of past grandeur. Decline of civilization(s) and of the New World! In Belles-lettres, she remembered having spent a year in the French nineteenth century. That's what they made us see most easily. Mistake in route? Mistake in date? Here we were stuck with the very elite of society forever harking back to, immersed in French patriotic and nostalgic themes.

The elite is two faced.

Whose pawn is this, where'll he go, where'll she go?

*Whom will she repudiate? The life of a girl at the bar, mar-
riageable girl, licensed for kids or the FFFFrench nineteenth
century? Two faced, the slap, neither one nor the other, both
one and the other, make one, turn your back on the other,
accept the one to undo it, unstitch it, to strip it without
slackening. The centre of gravity pee-poo in the pot. Hides in
the glass, goes to sleep between two deserts, this is the way
she defends herself.*

(55–57)

Narrative strategy: Cross that liminal area between how the barmaid
looks and what she thinks; cross it constantly; bring the interior into
jarring discontinuity with the exterior.

~ ~ ~

In the patriarchal scheme of values what is considered useless (i.e.,
doesn't serve the hierarchy of competitive male interests) equates with
what is worthless or undesirable, and then, by a kind of rapid de-
escalation, with what is unclean or dirty, as Dorothy Dinnerstein so
tellingly elaborates in *The Mermaid and the Minotaur* when she speaks
of domestic labour (cleaning bathrooms and babies' bums), and how
most men see it as "women's work."

According to the social norms of what is desirable in the market economy we live under, beautiful girls with well-toned, well-tanned young
bodies, whose hands seem never to have wielded toilet brushes,
whose attractively made-up faces seem never to have yelled at

children—these are what sell cars. Housing project mothers don't, bag ladies don't, disabled women don't—the list could go on and on. Only those whose bodies show no sign of wear and tear, who manage to look in "mint condition," like the cars they pose beside. Obviously, what is desirable, i.e., marketable, what is offered as ready for use, is being defined exclusively by the patriarchal gaze that sees in "brand new" car and "brand new woman" (child prostitute, for instance) the seductiveness of its own power. Brand new/brand name—a guarantee of quality for the user.

Gail Scott's fiction often plucks images of the feminine from popular culture and explores their impact on a young woman's struggle to salvage a positive image of herself. Like Théoret she moves rapidly between external image and internal assessment, combined with memory and its storytelling in "Main Bride Remembers Halifax":

> *Thank God the train was moving. Her pale reflection in the window reminded her of something. Pulling out her lipstick, she changed her image from the natural look obligatory for a debutant to a cosmopolitan '40s-style woman. By simply darkening the mouth in a firm and generous stroke of red red lipstick. So that even the pink-shirred strapless evening gown she wore was transformed from demure to worldly. There she was: maybe not so marriageable. But bold, confident of her sexuality to the point of devastating. A woman who could do anything with a man because so distanced from the act she was putting on.*
>
> *She smiled at the image. Suddenly remembering this persona'd been first conceived by a dusty baseball diamond*

back in Halifax. When the dusks in larger villages and smaller cities still gave the illusion there was space to become anything you wanted. Standing there, allegedly to watch the boys play, she was in reality sizing up the other girls. Eleanor P., whose father openly slept with women, including Eleanor's girlfriends, was overweight; Francoise M., whose father beat her mother, was beautiful but bitchy. There was la tristesse of Sandra M., manhandled in other ways by her old man. Compared to them, she, Adèle (a pseudonym inspired by a French poet's daughter) felt very fortunate in terms of family consequences: her father was mostly absent. It was up to her to ensure this situation continued. Keep a distance by putting on an act. Right there and then she determined to speak only with a deep throaty voice: a means used by courtesans in French novels. Also, they were never fixed on one affection.

The problem was a palatable way to make a living.

(1992, 102–3)

Narrative strategy: Take the patriarchal images of a woman's social currency, recontextualize them from within women's unspoken experience, theatricalize them to falsify their image-making. Amplify role-options by cross-referencing reality with fiction.

~ ~ ~

What is invidious about the dominant scheme of values is that the marketable/desirable gets defined as the feminine norm every woman is supposed to live up to. So where does this situate the ample range of women who do not fit this narrow definition? Where does it leave our self-image, not to mention our desire, our perceptions of reality, our truths? In the dark of our own heads, with the cultural trash that shapes self-doubt when we find ourselves outside the norm. And here i do mean trash as refuse, the unusable.

In any act of salvaging, one has to look closely at the so-called damaged goods. Both on the level of concept and on the level of verbal association. One has to put into question the scale of values that determines what is trash and what is of value.

The Flirtations, an openly gay American *a capella* group, sing "we are living in wartime," and their "we" embraces more than the gay community. The chronic underfunding of medical and other support to AIDS sufferers who at first were dismissed as "only" gay (i.e., expendable members of society) is one aspect of this war. There are others. Child sexual abuse, both privately at home and on the streets in child prostitution, as well as domestic violence against women have left the shadowy area of social taboo to stand in the spotlight of public discussion. Accompanying this, the increasing poverty of single mothers and their children, who have somehow become "invisible" as the upper middle-class standard of living increases. Now we know the scale of this war we are living in the midst of. Though incidents like the Montreal massacre erupt to dramatize it in terrifying clarity, it is a war that goes on daily in much more insidious, and more dangerous, form. It is a war of names, a war of values, a war of realities so different as to be almost unrecognizable to each other. The anonymous hands that chalk a feminist faculty member's door with "kill" slogans are as monstrously inhuman to us as autonymous women must be to the mind behind that chalk. How even address the gulf between these two conceptions of the human?

For women, this is our immediate environment and our history, in the making as we live it.

Marlene Nourbese Philip is keenly aware of history for additional reasons, filtered as it is through the stifled pain of slavery at the beginning of Black experience of the Americas. Her poetry moves with a careful awareness of how this sets her at odds with the cultural freight English words carry—words like "history" and "memory." In "She Tries Her Tongue, Her Silence Softly Breaks," each line registers her particular angle of difference as she builds a series of assertions she can live with.

> *Hold we to the centre of remembrance*
> *that forgets the never that severs*
> *word from source*
> *and never forgets the witness*
> *of broken utterances that passed*
> *before and now*
> *breaks the culture of silence*
> *in the ordeal of testimony;*
> *in the history of circles*
> *each point lies*
> *along the circumference*
> *diameter or radius*
> *each word creates a centre*

> *circumscribed by memory . . . and history*
> *waits at rest always*
>
> *still at the centre*
>
> (96)

Lyric strategy: With repetition and litanic running-on (over the cliff of the right margin), counter that state of being circumscribed by silence; note how each word of testimony will create its own live centre, even while "history / waits" as always (with its double "still") there at the dead centre of all circles. No way out for those who read you with attention. Specifically, no way out of reading Nourbese Philip's condemnation of how white Canada, through the tacit racism embedded in its standard English, severs Black immigrants from their West Indies "tongue," their mother-dialect, and the history that dialect speaks.

~ ~ ~

If women of colour have to regularly run the street gauntlet of "black bitch" and other affronts to their personhood, the racism of these verbal attacks adds a further painful dimension to a layer of misogyny at work in Canada's mainstream culture, a misogyny that can be understood as the genderized version of colonialism, the will to supremacy. In an article titled "Sexual Detective," Brian Fawcett describes the typical sexual conditioning he acquired as an adolescent in the small town culture of northern B.C. Through discussions with older men about sex, he was initiated into a dominant male view of women as sex objects, used for sex and therefore "dirty." He talks about the "uncleanness" that characterized their references to women, the off-hand remarks about dirty holes, filthy pussy, etc. His article works to undo such conditioning in men, but it presents damning evidence of an archaically negative layer in the way women are viewed in mainstream culture.

Confronted with this, we can resort to theory and find the analogue in Freud's description of women as anatomical and cultural damaged goods. Human beings lacking a penis and so lacking the dominant cultural signifier of the phallus which ascribes value and would, if we only had it, make us complete human beings, "men" in that universal sense. So here we are, women as "holes," as minus-men, "-men" with "wo(e)" for a prefix. Not wholly human, something unholy.

This, in short, is the "bottom" line of the cultural trash we've inherited. That if women are seen as already mutilated in the patriarchal scheme of things, then it's not such a big step to mutilating us further, even murdering us when we seem to be acquiring more than we "deserve." And if massacring women for their access to a traditionally male preserve of education is yet too rare an event to generalize from, we need only look at the verbal climate of sexual slur that surrounds us daily.

The question returns, as it does in daily life each time we're confronted with it: how to salvage a sense of self-worth in all of this? How to see, and then see *through,* this pervasive conceptual junk? The play that feminist salvagers resort to can be vividly serious as it makes light of colloquial usage. In "The Breasts Refuse," Betsy Warland takes on the "red rag" of a casual slur and salvages her own terrain:

he belittles "on the rag?"
he castigates "rag, rag!"

she sees red

then later
dis-covers
red rag is
"Old slang for tongue"
and his mean-ing
is changed

she puts on some ragtime
smiles dancing on her face

                                        red tape

his word is law
(archaic, "to bullyrag")

her monthly red-handedness
her tongue's teleology

language, he maintains, is neuter

she looks it up—
neuter, ne-, no + uter, either (see ne, see kwo-),
ne- no, deny + kwo-, alibi
language no alibi!
she muses on his red herring

as language becomes
new-to-her

(1990, 22–23)

Lyric strategy: Take words at "face value" in their idiomatic currency, and, through an investigation of their sources and cognates, subvert their negative meaning, trace an other linguistic history that generates affirming ones.

~ ~ ~

Feminist writing, when it destroys the reader's expectations of normative language use, form and genre, can be seen as a subversion of conventional/patriarchal reality embedded in those expectations. Such reality, which mainstream culture sets up as *the* reality, denies, derides or deranges many aspects of the realities women actually live. Salvaging a woman-specific reality involves not just picking up the trashed remains of what we experience and putting together some facsimile of the normal. It involves rescuing splinters, even whole logs (logos) of the dismissed, our dis-*ms.*'d, from the shores of the inarticulate as workable wood for a new assemblage, a different cultural vision.

What if we salvage value from the trashed by taking that letter "w" for woman, which is already a letter with more than one in it, double "v," symbol for the pudenda—what if we take "w" as the sign of our potential, our bonding (not our bondage) as women? Our inscription as subjects of our own experience, not that reduced object of the male gaze—"holes." And what if we add that empowering initial "w" to our cultural absence, turning "hole" into whole, into collective presence, as Gail Scott does, salvaging a positive, **w**+hole, from the sexist slur for women (74)? Writing ourselves in to as large a vision as we might imagine.

In a new system of values we will have to deface the old reductive terms in order to inscribe new values generated out of that whole-with-a-"w" we feel ourselves capable of becoming. Values that are doubly inscribed with a sense of the wholeness of our individual being, as well as the well-being of our relations with other women from whom we derive a positive sense of our worth. For when we gather together in whatever ways we do, at women's caucus meetings, over kitchen tables, in the streets at demonstrations, in healing circles or even in print, joining our words in support of one another's visions for a different kind of future, we salvage our own worth and realize our power to create an other-wise economy. An economy wise in the value of connectedness.

Prose itself, the very stuff of writing, can offer a metaphor for such connectedness in its syntactic relations. In her prose poem sequence, "Ultrasounds," Nicole Brossard celebrates the power of *la prose* in light of "her" (rather than its) potential for just such "liaison." "Beautiful liaison": word by word, image by image, woman by woman:

> The truth of prose lies in the filth of cliches, its essence in a
> sudden opacity that awakens our sleeping meanings. That
> being so, prose offers its epochs like so many mirrors, scripts
> and generations to ease the reading of the values and emo-
> tions that enter into the composition of our sexual parts. It is
> therefore used for various purposes, the main ones being to

recover the memory of childhood, to observe the slow motion, movements and folds of feeling, and to shape the desiring self. Prose says that nothing really dies. *Prose absorbs the shadow of our tears, absorbs part of our lives, the better to offer them to us in the munificence and spareness of our first visions.*

Prose, prose, here is the essential word of a happy liaison between the abundant nature of the I and the copious imagination that enters into the composition of the real. Beautiful liaison, to which many women are indebted for a glimpse of the possibility that their sexual parts are more numerous than is usually thought. Prose, prose, starting with the ear, that sexed pearl (the ear being sensitive to a very wide variety of sounds, it easily welcomes the most strange propositions, the most bold words, provided they are accompanied by certain images known for the pleasure they provoke) where the secret leaning of our assertions takes over from the thread of narratives. Prose is tenacious, little comes together without her.

(23–24)

Narrative strategy in its broadest sense: write to real-ize (make real), in the way our words connect and add to one another, the rich composition of the female imaginary as it opens up the real. The "copious," the "munificent": this *and* this, both, *and* this . . .

~ ~ ~

Unlike the "either/or" construction of western thought, which is based on scarcity and exclusion, "both/and" thinking springs from an intuition of abundance and works inclusively with the sense that there is enough (room) for all. "Both/and" thinking attributes value to both sides of the categorical slant. Or as Carol Gilligan puts it when discussing women's ethics, this kind of thinking is "contextual" and "contingent on sustaining connection" (19; 59). Connection is broken as soon as devaluation enters in, as soon as one entity is considered valuable and another written off. We know this, but sustaining contextual thinking in the face of the constant barrage of privileged dichotomies that construct hierarchical thought can render us at times speechless. Yet if we think of ourselves as not alone but joined in a network of salvagers, we can work to undo the mono-vision of the repressive culture that surrounds us, subvert its hierarchies and see other-wise with a vision that embraces rather than excludes.

There is, in fact, an abundance of subversive feminist writing finding its way into print in this country. The following is by no means an exhaustive list of additional names.

In Quebec feminist writers have created a new literary genre by crossing narrative with theoretical analysis and poetic language. Not only France Théoret and Nicole Brossard, but others including Louky Bersianik, Louise Cotnoir and Louise Dupré write fiction/theory. In English-Canadian poetry, writers like Libby Scheier and Di Brandt turn the negative "hysterical" into an ecstatic excessive line, rewriting patriarchal takes on women from an unholy and more holistic perspective. Lola Lemire Tostevin, Penn Kemp, Jam Ismail delight in word play, using it to inscribe a polyvalence of meaning or elide the dominance of unilingual meaning by punning between languages.

Dionne Brand and Sky Lee fuse oral and written dialects, infusing social commentary with a profound sense of women's historic oppression in their respective cultures. Like Québécoise writers, Erin Mouré and Janice Williamson transgress old genre borders, crossing privileged genres such as poetry, fiction and critical theory with socalled secondary ones—journal entries, dream-narratives, recipes, letters, family anecdote. Mary Meigs crosses novelistic portraits of women close to her with self-reflection and the detail of a painter's journal as she explores the implications of autobiography as a genre. Aboriginal writers like Jeannette Armstrong and Lee Maracle erase boundaries between traditional Native oratory and contemporary social critique in their writing of poetry, non-fiction, and fiction.

There are many more women writing in these ways than those i have named, more coming up who are just publishing their first books. In fact, there is a wonderful colloquy between them, and this writing of women to women in itself proposes a major cultural upheaval.

l-r Daphne Marlatt, Gail Scott, and Louise Cotnoir at the Dialogue Conference, York University, 1981.

bp Nichol and George Bowering at Simon Fraser University, 1982.

Now you can fly
between
Sydney and Adelaide
without leaving
the ground

The
and

ROBYN ELPHICK

Daphne Marlatt and Betsy Warland on their reading tour, Australia, 1986.

EVELYN FINGARSON

l-r Betsy Warland, Lee Maracle, Jeannette Armstrong, and Surjeet Kalsey at the Telling It Conference, 1986.

reprinted with permission of Press Gang Publishers EVELYN FINGARSON

l-r Viola Thomas, Joy Kogawa, Louise Profeit laBlanc, Sky Lee, and Barbara Herringer at the Telling It Conference, November 1986.

Phyllis Webb and Sharon Thesen at the tribute to Phyllis Webb, Western Front, Vancouver, 1992.

Sharon Thesen at Western Front, Vancouver, 1992.

Smaro Kamboureli at Western Front, Vancouver, 1992.

Nicole Brossard in Dublin, 1996.

ALAN MARLATT

l-r Daphne Marlatt, Betsy Warland, and Kit Marlatt at Warm Beach, Washington, 1987.

DAPHNE MARLATT

Sky Lee and son Nathan on Salt Spring Island, 1993.

DAPHNE MARLATT

Jam Ismail on Salt Spring Island, 1993.

GORDON MCKILLOP

Daphne Marlatt and Bridget MacKenzie with Suka, 1994.

Athens. May 10. 92

It was raining when we got here, which was fine—nice to feel rain on my face again—all the orange trees are half in blossom, half in fruit so the streets in our neighbourhood (Koukaki, below the Acropolis) are incredibly fragrant in the wet, even through the murk of traffic. B. says the fragrance makes her want a cup of jasmine tea.

We've found a pension, cheaper than the hotel, are learning to read Greek (capital letters anyway) & speak a few phrases. Took our things to the laundromat a few doors down, to a man who does it himself & sent it back all neatly folded in a paper package—with somebody else's towel included. Tomorrow we leave the mainland.

~ ~ ~

at sea en route to Lesbos. May 11.

Sailing in the shellpink light of late afternoon on (of course!) the *Sapfo*, past the peninsula east of Piraeus, its cliffs, white gulls, white mother boats all pinkish in this light—past the temple of Poseidon, absent column in silhouette, a marker merely—sad that the old gods are no longer believed in, their energies lost—

Later: stood at the rail with B. for a long time as we sailed into a darkening world, north, away from the sunset, heading for the Cyclades & then Chios where we dock at 3 a.m.—sky still the palest pink, though stars out, big dipper overhead—stretches of light & darker swatches on the mirror-calm surface of sea—odd patches of foam (from boats passed on before us?), dark hills very dim in the distance with a few, very few & solitary, lights—thought of the heroes returning home to bonfires (acclaim or loss, Theseus & his black sails)—except for our ship & these few lights, there is only a darkening & indefinable distance, hard to see where the horizon is in all the mistiness—very serene, spacious, large— a bardo state, perhaps, one of the states after death, the mind-stream

flying illimitable distance, not worried or attached, only a sense of
movement & halflight, space, gliding itself the be-all—

~ ~ ~

Skala Erissou. May 19.

after this prolonged quiet time, the ruins of Sappho, traces of her
everywhere, even the Burnett book [Three Archaic Poets] stumbled on
by chance in a local gift-shop, how marvellously Burnett talks about her
school: "once enrolled, a girl enjoyed the same membership in an extra-
communal band that she might have found in an initiation class, for
this elitist circle was evidently licensed by the community, just as the
older puberty groups had been. It had a place within the public order as
a discrete social organism where society's usual rules for a time did
not prevail"—impossible for us to imagine in our current social order
which puts young people through a stage of peer-enforced homophobia
at school

she taught the girls to know their own emotions & to objectify them in
song, "courting one another to the tune of their lyres"—& how that
phase of their lives taught them the erotic in the largest sense: "she
offers her girls the memory of a time where music, ritual and fleshly
passion mingled smoothly together and an almost mythical beauty
resided in carnal love, for in her song-made world there is no dissonance
between beauty that is spiritual and beauty that is animal"

all this & the blue of the Aegean, its constant sounds here, a
concatenation of water falling onto rock & soughing out, pebbles rolling,
pause, then a new, another breaking splash that gathers as it runs along
the shore—most of all, that lively scent in the dry grass of oregano,
chamomile, other herbs we don't recognize—white goats under the
moonlight—&, Sappho's heritage, the definiteness of the older women
who carry a sense of their own worth

—anyway, after this prolonged visit (even our hotel is, of course, Hotel Sapfo) it's difficult to be immersed again in the busy-work of travelling, its myriad details: our tenuous car-rental arrangement, driving back to Mitilene (if it works), agreeing on payment & then will we have enough cash to get ferry tickets? sailing—what to do in Piraeus for 12 hours with our bags, & can we get tickets to sail for Iraklion that night?—through all of which i find it hard to remember:

"In her creed, a delicate sumptuousness (abrosuna . . .) accurately enjoyed, gives both an outward brilliance and an inner splendour to one's love of life"

~ ~ ~

Her(e) in the Labyrinth:
Reading/Writing Theory

*In September 1992 the Association for Canadian Studies held a confer-
ence in Saint-Jovite, Quebec, titled Theoretical Discourse in the Canadian
Intellectual Community. I was asked to speak with Québécoise writer Louky
Bersianik on a panel moderated by critic Patricia Smart. My text from that
occasion appeared in* Canada: Theoretical Discourse, *edited by Terry Goldie,
Carmen Lambert and Rowland Lorimer. It has been substantially rewritten here.*

The labyrinthine structure of the text, which may be entered but not
easily traversed—text whose passageways pose no easy passage, wind
back on each other and forward, or end abruptly in confining walls—
text a woman is finding her way through, hesitant which way to
proceed, glancing at images off walls which offer dubious reflection at
best—maze of dead ends (in which she finds herself?)

(Starting again) this labyrinthine structure of the text, not imposed but
improvised—a work of penetration possible? to what end? Ariadne
caught in the symbolic code of her culture that posits her absent,
outside it, looking for a way in—woman in process, rereading, writing
herself in as subject—in ruin / in a ruin—these meandering passageways—slippage.

~ ~ ~

Being asked for the title of a text before writing it feels like being asked to find the heart of the labyrinth before even setting foot inside the door. (Of course, time constraints in organizing a conference . . . funding requirements . . .) Linguistic requirements: Theoretical Discourse. Feminist Narratology. Postcolonial Stratagems. The sensation of certain walls beginning to close. Ariadne on the outside wondering how to find a way (her way) in.

Images, she thinks. Labyrinth a structure of interconnecting passages. What is the relationship of poetic text to theory, or of imagining, that thinking through images, to rational argument? Imagining Theory as Poetic Text? Only a hopeful banner draped over the entrance. What she wants to work is her own passage, serially lost in the traverse of language-working-text where walls, the images thereon, keep shifting ground depending on perspective—no orthodox (single-doxa) compass, no universal destination, only the thread of where she's been travelling, travailing, unravelling behind (her).

How posit theory outside the body writing it? The bios of auto graphing its reading of the world. From where (it) lives.

Acquainted at least with the idea of the labyrinth i flew to Crete.

~ ~ ~

Knossos, Phaestos, Mallia. These storied structures, labyrinths of glaring light and cryptlike shadow. A *complete cosmos of light yet mystery* (Papapostolou 28). Walls with their blue dolphins, blue rivers, brown *rhyton* bearers and death-pale dancing girls.

This *Lily-Prince*, this tauro-acrobat soaring over the head of a bull, this *Goddess* with staring eyes who is lifting the snakes in her hands . . .

Artefacts, concrete things made by hands alive some three to four thousand years ago, separated from our curious touch by sheets of glass, they stand indubitably here a few inches from us in museum stillness, lifted forever out of living context.

Impossible not to wonder: what was their immediate context, shaped by fingers active with intent, visionary in fresh paint or clay? In a different light, perhaps a different weather, certainly before earthquake, marauding desolation and the erosion of centuries, not to mention world-views.

~ ~ ~

If the text carries the traces of the body and its passage through place/time, then it is marked by memory, that dubious compass needle veering under the magnetic pull of the present as it reads a fabulous store of imprints in body tissue.

Ariadne's magic ball of memory-thread unwinding forward in narrative —so you can find your way *back,* she said, standing at the entrance with its end in her hand.

186

~ ~ ~

Labyrinth, first reading-encounter: "Theseus had not taken five steps before he lost sight of Ariadne; and in five more his head was growing dizzy. But still he went on, now creeping through a low arch, now ascending a flight of steps, now in one crooked passage and now in another, with here a door opening before him, and there one banging behind, until it really seemed as if the walls spun round, and whirled him round along with them" (Hawthorne 239).

The push of narrative forward through the clenching and unclenching of syntax, passage repeating with variation—a labyrinthine trace.

~ ~ ~

I flew to Crete, or rather we sailed by ferry from Piraeus. Two women entering the remains of one part of their complex cultural tradition, bearing in mind if not body the latest Western translation of an old emblem: *labrys,* double-axe of an ancient dynasty of Minos kings, now the emblem of lesbian sexuality.

Our ferry docks early, the streets of Iraklion just beginning to stir. Two literate illiterates, we drag our bags uphill, half-awake, wondering if we're going the right way/which way to a relatively quiet hotel through this maze of signs in unremembered Greek. Breakfast first, you say as we come upon a small plaza with tables outside, no waiter but a few seated people, one promising door open. Tantalizing smell of coffee, fresh bread, white tablecloth. We seat ourselves at the table in the same postures we use at home. Sigh of relief. Traces of the familiar misting over the uninterpretable clarity of the strange.

~ ~ ~

We see the real life of the Minoan world only in the mirror rites of the dead (Wunderlich 137).

Mirror, light reflected not through but back: a curious figure in this context. Real life (the life of the living) to be read in the life of the dead, centuries later. Vases, jewellery, weapons, cups, seals, shrines, frescoes . . . these things they took with them into the underworld, that world on the other side of the mirror, a world we no longer know how to read, except in our own image.

~ ~ ~

Travelling reinscribes the experience of ghostifying that emigration is. The people, streets, rooms, plants, speech, foods of home made shadows merely, under the increasing substantiality of this which surrounds us. Home shifts, becomes synonymous with an empty hotel room rendered gradually familiar with our things, our smells, our habits. While that which was most familiar wanes, difficult to conjure in full. Even my bank-account number fades (posing a cash problem)—as if i had walked into the labyrinth with no thread back

188

and found myself with that bull-fear: to disappear without a trace.

~ ~ ~

. . . the monstrousness of selfhood is intimately embedded within the question of female autobiography (Johnson 154).

~ ~ ~

Labyrinth, second reading-encounter:
> . . . built by Daedalus, an artist
> Famous in building, who could set in stone
> Confusion and conflict, and deceive the eye
> With devious aisles and passages. As Maeander
> Plays in the Phrygian fields, a doubtful river,
> Flowing and looping back and sends its waters
> Either to source or sea, so Daedalus
> Made those innumerable windings wander,
> And hardly found his own way out again. . . .

(Ovid 186)

The winding back and forth of verse, its echo-syllabics repeating "-er." And (Maeander) the usual motifs: confusion and conflict, devious passages, doubtful flowing and looping back . . . state of being lost, of not-knowing. Fear of no return.

Daedalus created the labyrinth to house the Minotaur, that hungry monster at its heart. To be lost therein is to be devoured.

~ ~ ~

Side by side in hot museum stillness, we gaze at a stone sarcophagus from Aghia Triada with its sacrificial bull trickling blood into a bucket and the usual procession of priests moving up from a line of waiting animals. There's a *labrys,* you point out, see it by the altar, with a bird on it? There's something about that combination, i remember, finding the page in the guidebook. Oh, it represents the epiphany of the goddess.

Epiphany, you muse. All we get are glimpses, just glimpses of how it must have been for them.

Outside at a sidewalk café, picking at slippery packages of dolmades which roll away in their fragrant lemon oil from under the tines of our forks, we wonder where *labrys* comes from, why *r* moved from pre-y to post-y in labyrinth. House of the Double Axe.

And were they real axes, i mean functional ones, or were they a sort of 3-D image?

(What about the image, a theory of images, of what the image renders present?)

Robert Graves describes the *labrys* as the waxing and waning moon, you know, the crescents, joined back to back.

Joined back to back? Not much fun, you grimace. A drop of oil slid-
ing into the hollow beneath your lower lip glints in the light as you
angle your head slightly and grin.

(Theory of what the image leaves out?)

~ ~ ~

Sir Arthur Evans, reading ruin upon ruin by the light of his British
imagination, reconstructs with cement, repaints, designates appropri-
ately palatial names, *restoring* the palace of Knossos to its pre-
devastation grandeur. Courts and Lobbies, King's Megaron, Queen's
Megaron, Queen's Lavatory . . . (?)

*. . . the desire to create a being like oneself—the autobiographical desire par
excellence.* (Johnson 146).

Entering a male lineage of readings that leaves Ariadne standing
outside, we climb like so many others in the full sun, guidebook in
hand, abstracted, staring at black bars and squares on a page. All
around us knots of people reading aloud in other languages. Tentative
stepping, checking at every turn with print (the authorized version).
Dominant symbolic code colours what we see. The West Court, yes,
we came through that, past the Porter's Lodge and Guardroom (put in
quotation marks, keeping in mind that these, like the Caravanserai,
are guesses rendered reliable by the guides' assertive voices). Up the
Corridor of the Procession—which turn will take us into the
Propylaia? Which empty cubicle of stone is the Myceanean Megaron

when we're lost, staring at print that won't translate us into body-habitable space?

~ ~ ~

In the space of theory for the woman writing, terms blur, move in and out of one another, despite what she feels is the sensory concreteness of the image, its very "sensibleness" (which still is not quite the same as having both feet on the ground). Further afield, imagining sprouts wings or perhaps fins, neither this nor that, a somewhat fishy activity, makes up, reads in, transforms. Despite calls for an imaginative approach (to theory, let's say), imagining can scarcely be invoked in the same breath as intellectual rigour.

She, the theorizing poet, recognizes that imagining undermines doxa, the authorized line of descent which legitimates theory. It's no longer a matter of, as Virginia Woolf wrote, not knowing Greek. But standing on the other side of the symbolic: on the absent ground of her literal.

~ ~ ~

Standing out on the street with our bags once again, we argue about who will venture in this time to ask for a double bed. It's easier to ask if one of us remains outside, invisible. Bed: *krevatee*. Double: *theeplo*—from two, *theeo* (but don't say *theeo;* that's for twin beds). At least it's

better than Italian when we had to ask for a *matrimoniale*. O our
unsacrosanct, our unauthorized relations.

~ ~ ~

. . . to identify the act of this reading as the enabling subjectivity of another
poetics, a poetics attached to gendered bodies that may have lived in history
(Miller 1986, 288).

Arachne, Ariadne. Go on living in us.

~ ~ ~

In the lineage of the labyrinth, a dispute of readings: Evans sees his
East wing a royal palace busy with accoutrements to the life of priest-
king and consort: its Stonecutters' Workshop, its Schoolroom for
training scribes, its bathtubs and Lavatory and Court of the Stone
Spout with settling tanks of rainwater for laundry . . .

In Wunderlich's reading, all "sham," all a mirror reflection of the real
thing. He notes the cups of shining bronze are only clay, thin as dolls'
ware. Heavily embossed gold vases merely soapstone leafed over. And
those double axes? So fine a single blow would bend them.
Something we don't notice, standing as we are outside glass museum
cases, persuaded by illusion.

In this "curious sham world we encounter in the Cretan palaces," (Wunderlich 155) he reads the provisioning of a magnificent tomb with grave-goods. Or rather a mortuary-temple, place of worship, its bathtubs and complex system of water pipes constructed for embalming not laundry. As for those "magazines" of wide-mouthed *pithoi*, huge jars? They were used for storing corpses not cooking oil. While below in the deepest most ornate chambers ("The King's Megaron," "the Queen's") sat the royally embalmed on thrones contrived to keep their bodies upright.

Traces of a more physical approach to dying. Elaborate tracings around the untraceable.

~ ~ ~

Stones swim in the heat. This ransacked world of the dead we suddenly want to exit, driven with a need to find trees, bliss in the cicada shrill of wings announcing their presence.

Seated on Cretan earth, our backs against fallen stone, we realize how thirsty we are. It's all this talk of empty water pipes, you laugh. Russet-blonde hairs on your arm glint as your fingers find mine. I imagine the slow crinkle of hairs under my tongue, the liquid meander it would leave along your arm, particles of dust and salt, your skin's hot taste in my mouth.

~ ~ ~

The human brain is constructed to make mental images of the information it receives from outside, but it does not detect all of the information that makes up the world. First of all, our senses are insensitive to much of it. . . . Moreover, we do not pay attention to all of the information that is actually detected by our senses; our brains filter out and ignore much of it. . . .

There are thus frequent gaps in our mental image of the real world, where large pieces seem to be missing, and so our minds invent connections that help us to make sense of the whole. . . . Every child, as it grows up, repeats this process of mental imaging of the world, and many of the unexplained gaps are filled in by myths or beliefs passed down from one generation to the next. This is a central part of the process of cultural transmission (Clark 16–17).

~ ~ ~

Whose story is the story of the labyrinth? Not Ariadne's. Only a narrative figure, she offers, she is, the thread between puzzle-setter Daedalus and puzzle-solver Theseus who will later abandon her on Naxos.

Her not here. Because she is in that ghost world on the other side of the mirror of representation.

But after all, the magic ball was Ariadne's, given to her long before Theseus. Unfolding clew to her own passage in, and out again. Loopy, looping passage of narrative she holds in her hand. If she would only read/write from where she stands, bringing the outside in with her, confronting the monstrousness of her unauthorized selfhood.

~ ~ ~

To write from where we stand, her(e) in the labyrinth . . .

~ ~ ~

Having reached the Queen's Megaron, we turn and look back at the entrance, at the bright fresco above it. Standing together, how do we read with eyes imprinted with other axes, orcas breaking the surface of Pacific waters, this wall we face, this fresco underground in a Minoan megaron where dolphins swim, submerged in a light space dark invades, as if in a cave? Forward and back, forward and back, blue dolphins, blue and knowing-eyed.

Do we read the physical pleasures of a people in harmony with their locale? Or the sacred colour of guides, transformative, in a world of the dead?

Or both: in the gap between, the image swings both ways, admitting what *or* sets outside.

~ ~ ~

The relationship of poet to text: the imposssibility of *not* reading through bios when she is the already dead, the long absented . . .

Keeping her hand in, waving, wav*her*ing through walls of the already read, reaching for traces of another woman's hand, vivid and present, to write her way here.

London. Oct. 6. 93

Dear Mary*,

Such a lovely note from you in Kingsbury—thank you so much. Now i hear from Betsy you're back in Montreal & i'm glad you two had such a good time together. I'm looking forward very much to reading the transcript of her interview with you when it's done. What a fine idea of hers that was.

So here i am in London as writer-in-residence, which seems rather strange. I feel underwater here, the surfaces where wind, sea & sky freshen each other are missing. What strikes me as oddest is that the earth has no smell—even when Betsy & i walked by the river during her visit on the weekend, it simply smelled musty & well-used. Oh dear, i'm such an inveterate West Coaster—it's because i can't stand being away from the sea for very long. And i do miss all that wet fragrance of the rainforest. But i have a small & comfortable apartment (entertaining Betsy here as a "guest" over the weekend felt odd & touching, but we had some good time together & i do feel more settled now).

The people in the English Dept. have been very kind, giving me more writing time than i deserved in September. Which was ironic, because i went into a deep depression about my writing, most particularly the novel [Taken] i've been working on. Have temporarily abandoned it (at least "temporarily" has now sneaked into that sentence). It seems to be falling far short of what i want it to be. Having just read Sara Suleri's wonderful autobiography of her family, Meatless Days, my portraits of these fictionalized personages who are partly my parents seem much too thin, too one-dimensional. The despair is poor memory (especially of those early years). How to dredge up from the backwaters what i so insistently & for so many years tried to drown so that i could become Canadian: non-imperial, "guiltless" (i realize this is a neurosis Anglo-Canadians share, & a personal fetish too no doubt).

At least in the hiatus i've been working on a poem, the first in a couple of years, & that feels good. One of my "women & island" poems, using some lines in translation from Renée Vivien. The way the Sapphic tradition keeps surfacing fascinates me.

* Mary Meigs

How is your book with Ruth coming along? I wish i was coming to Montreal so we could have one of those long chats.

~ ~ ~

London. Oct. 17. 93.

Nancy K. Miller, succinct as usual: "the fictions of desire behind the desiderata of fiction are masculine" ["Emphasis Added: Plots & Plausibilities in Women's Fiction"]

stewing around in all this, having lost my nerve, just when i have to speak, to classes, to the Theory Center, to Women's Studies, not to mention the invitations coming in from other universities—

trying to understand why this crisis, this sense of illegitimacy—not an academic & right now barely feel like a writer either—

the question is: is self-representation possible in a language & in literary forms so encoded by patriarchal constructs?

Margaret Homans in her essay in *Signs* re the French writers who "accept the premise that language & experience are co-extensive also understand language to be a male construct whose operation depends on women's silence & absence"—she goes even further: "Once female silence & death are represented in language, they cease to interfere with the text & become simply one more episode in a narrative than can cordon off their powerful disruptive effects"—not sure that's true of Duras' work which *is* disruptive on a subliminal level—

but it makes me think of my novel, the role of the scientific mother, or rather the re-sanctified role of the mother that science authorized in the 40s—& that E. enjoys (as an extension of her desire to become a nurse)—it's a position in the dominant discourse, amplified by wartime

calls for Australian nationalism: doing her patriotic duty as a mother—
which she resists, her ambivalence here—& all this disrupted (that sense
of disturbance) by news of atrocities, what is happening to the women
POWs, news of Petiot's female victims in occupied Paris—this constant
threat of erasure she senses

            —not a fiction, but a reflection of
something real in the culture—& behind it? the repressiveness of
language we can't break through?—such a despairing notion

but Homans also says that American writers assume "experience is
separable from language & thus that women are or can be in control of
language rather than controlled by it, making women capable of self-
representation"

            not sure about her Fr./Am. opposition
here—seems to me experience <u>can</u> occur outside of language (witness
meditation) but it can't be <u>communicated</u> outside of language, which
is what makes working with language so necessary—bending it, making
holes in it to let what isn't talked about, the darkness outside the
authorized circles of light, leak through—

            o how do you represent a self that is both
present & about-to-be-erased? or, to step outside self-focus for a
moment: how represent the largeness of context a self inhabits, so large
we can't see what actually <u>composes</u> it?

"Perform[ing] on the Stage of Her Text"

During my fall term as writer-in-residence at the University of Western Ontario in 1993, the Centre for the Study of Theory and Criticism asked me to speak on women's autobiography and feminism. These remarks formed the basis of a paper given a year later at the Second Autumn Summer School on the New Literatures in English at the University of Aachen in Germany. What follows is a further elaboration, prompted by the occasion of giving a lecture at the University of Victoria, spring 1997.

Memory + imagination = "fiction" (?)

To write autobiography is to remember, to dwell in (inhabit) the past, to go back, recall the very feel and smell of a place, the kinetics of an event, the actual words said—all these expectations we have of replay, as if facticity could make a past indelible forever. Yet we know how unreliable memory is, how subtly it alters without even conscious decision to do so, how much it invents.

Although my work is, to a large extent, autobiographical, i'd never thought of my books as autobiography. Perhaps because i came to writing through poetry and fiction. No matter how autobiographically based a piece of fiction is, it uses the mask of an other, even as tenuous an other as an unnamed narrator. And while poetry often arises from perceptions generated out of lived experience, these are moments only and they don't add up to the conventional story of a person's life with its beginning and, if not end, at least some sense of the actual shape of that life, with its sloughs and peak moments.

Autobiography, it seemed to me, involved rendering a full account of one's life. (To whom? and on what terms? were not questions that occurred to me then).

In 1988, i came across an essay by Nancy K. Miller titled "Women's Autobiography in France: For a Dialectics of Identification." In this essay she asks "what conventions . . . govern the production of a female self as *theater:* that which literally is given to be seen? How does a woman writer perform on the stage of her text?" (260). These questions cracked the usual watertight walls that separate genres and made me look at my own "production" of a female self.

This move away from an honest rendering to theatre had already been presaged for me in the writing of *Zócalo*, a prose work that occupied some transitional site between memoir and fiction. When my publisher asked me to describe it for back cover copy, i hadn't known what to call it. It couldn't be memoir, i thought, because it was written in the third person. On the other hand it was fictional only to the extent that i invented some of the dialogue in the wake of failed memory. Although much of it is written in the present tense, it was all composed in a sustained effort to remember a trip to Mexico months after it was over.

In her essay on memoir, "The Site of Memory," Toni Morrison writes, "[a]ll water has a perfect memory and is forever trying to get back to where it was. Writers are like that: remembering where we were, what valley we ran through, what the banks were like, the light that was there and the route back to our original place. It is emotional memory —what the nerves and the skin remember as well as how it appeared. And a rush of imagination is our 'flooding'" (119). In this lyrical articulation of how memory and imagination conspire, Morrison stresses terrain as the very stuff of memory. The immediate "siting" imagination leaps to, as if context were everything (and it is). Are we who we are because of where we've been? Does place, including the company present, actually stage identity so that identity takes its shape from it? It's not uncommon to experience oneself as different with different people or in different places, weathers, with different activities—is the me that slips into dream between lines of a novel late at night the same me that negotiates a crowded supermarket during the day?

These questions, only dimly articulated, prompted the writing of *Zócalo*. What intrigued me about writing it was how much more easily i could remember in the third person. As if this Yucatan journey had not only occurred in another place but to another person. I would ask myself how could that be? Surely i am the legitimate possessor of my memories, so why can't "i" unlock them at will? But "i" was doubtful about the authenticity of these memories and came up with very little, only bare outlines, a sketchy sense of this or that before a little voice intervened, "Are you sure that's how it was?" "She," however, was a different story—not so much *different* as another angle on the same story. As if this she, through whose eyes and nerves and skin everything filtered, could open onto the streets of Merida or the pathways of Uxmal like a camera lens, a performing eye/she whose active perception brought alive the feel and texture of these places populated by strangers walking and talking there on the brightly lit stage of the text. She was there with them, in the very writing of "she turns to him," "she watches them," "they climb onto the bus." She was there in those streets with Yo, who is himself a combination of first and third persons (*yo* meaning "i" in Spanish as well as a shortened form of Yoshio, a Japanese given name). Perhaps because "she" is more visible than "i" yet more anonymous since she does not even have the author's name to be linked to, let alone her own name in this text; she has less of a marked presence, less claim on truth and a greater range of what Morrison calls "emotional memory." It was possible to write this she from behind her eyes as if she were me, and paradoxically, it was only possible because i could see her out there in the midst of those streets, those rooms, those ruins, walking amidst all the others.

The uses of fiction: is it only in making strange that we see ourselves, that is, the patterning in what our perceptions note or what our consciousness habitually engages? obsessive motifs of thought? repeating questions?—by which we identify ourselves. Is it this that gradually comes clear on the stage of the text?

What intrigued me about Miller's questions was the way they abandon the notion of self-revelation, a notion that suggests there is an essential self the public curtains of disclosure will open on. She offers in its place the concept of the *performance* of a self. What does this imply? That self is what gets enacted in telling, under the stage lights of personal recollection and narration, against and with already read, already scripted notions of gender—and class, race, ethnic background. Multi-faceted refractions. Unravelling of roles across illumined and dark spaces. All of which, taken together, might construct the "truth" of what we call this self.

Accountability and Audience

From the internal world of the self (*auto-*) and its *bios*, the autobio-graphical moves toward the external world of the audience through -*graphy*, writing, making public. The self that is written is written with public accountability in mind: this has conventionally constituted the autobiographer's pact with her audience. To tell the truth, rather than fiction. To offer documentation, photo disclosure. These are the expectations readers bring. How has this affected women writing autobiography?

If in autobiography the private self has gone public, then this has his-torically involved women in a transgression of the conventional feminine gender role. Until the last few decades, a woman who went public in some sense de-feminized herself. She left the private domes-tic world, or to continue our theatrical metaphor, the audience seated anonymously in the dark where the spotlight was on others, and stepped into the bright lights of public scrutiny where she engaged in self-advertising, in "making a spectacle" of herself. Only fifty years ago Elizabeth Smart's parents tried to destroy all copies of *By Grand Central Station I Sat Down and Wept* that reached Canada. Even today any woman active in the public sphere knows that she is scrutinized on a double level, not just on the basis of her performance as a (fill in the blank: prime minister, news anchor, opera star) but also on the basis of her performance as a woman. Female autobiographers are read in a way that male autobiographers are not, as Nancy Miller notes: they are read as women, that is, according to deeply encoded social scripts for what constitutes femininity.

From puberty and the onset of an interest in women's images in advertising, a girl is encouraged to view herself in the light of that femininity and from outside her own subjectivity. I remember as a young teenager having to take the bus across town to the orthodontist's. Having your teeth straightened as a girl is clearly not only about the mechanics of chewing. It's also aimed at improving one's looks, one's marketability as a young woman. My particular orthodontist, a paternalistic and attractive man, tried to ameliorate the pain by fostering Hollywood fantasies of the end result. The boredom of that long bus ride magnified his words as i saturated myself with images of women models in the ads running just above the heads of other passengers. By the time i rose to get off the bus, the self-consciousness of trying to live up to those images would affect every move i made. Seeing myself from the outside, i froze in the image-making lens of the culture's gaze.

Anyone writing autobiography faces the question of how much to reveal of the private under the glare of public expectation that all will be revealed for the sake of "a good story." Even without giving in to this demand, in order to convey destiny (narrative momentum), achievement (dramatic action), even consistency of character, certain traits will be magnified, certain incidents repressed. In short the shaping hand of the self-narrator (a sleight of hand that approximates fiction) will fashion a unified persona to present to public view. Cultural expectation solicits this and enshrines it in the iconic phenomenon of the "great man." But a woman faces an additional problem: how does she tell the story of a self split by genderization into an object seen from the outside that often masks or stands at odds with what she experiences of her subjectivity. How does a woman tell the story of a self that hovers fictively on the threshold between subject and object?

Miller's notion of the performance of a self on the stage of her text provides space for this blurred entity to invent ways of speaking that feel truthful to its *ficticity* (a threshold word between facticity and fictionality). Getting close to articulating something i might recognize, i have to tunnel back to a place of not-knowing in order to narrate becoming. The phrases we ordinarily use for this revolve around things (Morrison's valley and banks and light), just as remembering or at least the effort to speak a memory revolves around naming. But that's not where immediacy is, the feel, the smell of it. It flares up in a movement that suggests the multiform shapes of other remembered moments, many of them strung together, kinematic (the kinetics of identity), cinematic if you will—not the snapshot self, that frozen thing.

This requires a peculiar kind of accountability that runs counter to the instant (quick-frozen) images of self the media peddle. Images which package out the mutable, inarticulate, blurred attributes of subjectivity. How does one convey the feel of being alive in this body at this moment in this place marked by, bearing traces of, the places, moments and people lived with, in and through to this point? Isn't self merely the juncture of such radii? This nameless point, this mobile spot that flares across the apparitional bodies of who we think we were or might be.

A curious dance, this writing of autobiography, between the private act of dreaming up (out of nowhere, nothing) and the public act of performing a recognizable self.

And then there is the stage on which a woman performs, a stage which has been constructed and illuminated by a long tradition of male concerns defining what is of public interest. The hallmark narratives of the genre she measures her life story against have, until recently, been those of great men with great deeds, occupiers of public space since ancient Athens. She struggles against the critical voices she has internalized, which decry her concerns as too personal, too insignificant (not historic enough, not large enough), just "women's issues." She lives out the fear behind her writing block: "i don't have anything worth saying." Or, to translate: what if the "self" revealed so (auto)graphically isn't worth the public space it takes up?

Caught again in that notion of a unitary and solid self which must somehow measure up to other so-inscribed selves. But the old monoliths of selfhood are crumbling apart in the acid rain of new theories of representation. This is a good time for women to be writing autobiography as we come to understand that the rational and singular self we were taught to emulate—so out of reach, so imperial in its sense of control—is a fantasy of the first order/First World. That the so-called "self" is a product of discourse, a fractured site of various identities and memberships on both sides of the rift of dominance. A site that shifts as point of view shifts. Interlocutive as much as locative.

Since Gilbert and Gubar, we know the source of our anxiety about female authority when we sit down to write. Since Cixous and Irigaray we know the necessity and the risks involved in writing a body marked female. Since Woolf and Spender and Olsen, who drew our attention to it, we hear the murmuring multilogue of literary mothers we write our way into.

Not enough has been said about how significant a sense of an immediate audience of women readers is for a woman writer. Such an audience breaks down the isolating specularity of her performance.

The almost bodily kinetics of identification radiate both ways across the footlights and the darkness beyond. I say both ways because a woman writer's sense of community with other women readers and writers means that she performs not for or with herself alone. The stage of her text is a shared stage, vitally resonant with voices that have often been inaudible until recently. These are the voices she resists and identifies with, voices that remind her of her affiliations on many levels, that push her toward a greater understanding of a process collectively engaged in: writing the complexity of our individual "selves," gender-marked as they are, fictive and mutable as we perform them, into the culture.

Female autobiography as a mutant genre

As they explore representations of identity, women writers often consciously play with the notion of the autobiographer's pact to tell the truth. They deliberately blur concepts of what constitutes fiction and what constitutes documentary or, more largely, non-fiction, and, in the process, come up with a genre that stands on the threshold of announcing itself as something different from either. Sidonie Smith goes so far as to suggest, in her coda to *A Poetics of Women's Autobiography*, that "'autobiography' no longer makes sense culturally" (174). Yet many contemporary works by women reveal a sustained interest in the way the story of a self intersects with a repertoire of larger cultural stories and, indeed, is shaped by a distinctively female recounting, even rewriting, of them.

Two relatively recent titles, *Frog Moon* by Lola Lemire Tostevin and

Captivity Tales: Canadians in New York by Elizabeth Hay, play with conventional genre expectations in different ways.

Tostevin's work is clearly defined as fiction by its author in a delicately worded statement at the back of the book: "*Frog Moon* is a novel whose characters are fictional; however, I would like to extend my gratitude to all pioneer voices that form the basis of its historical, legendary, and mythological chronology, especially my parents, Laurette and Achilles Lemire" (219). The reader remembers at that point that the narrator's father in the novel is also named Achilles. In fact his daughter Laura, the narrator, comments on the mythological aura surrounding his name as she introduces her English translation of the oral stories (part-legend, part-fact and certainly legendary within the family's own construction of its fragmented identity) which constitute his life-story and a large part of her own francophone heritage. Provoked to look up the author's bio, the reader discovers that, like Laura, Tostevin was born to Franco-Ontarian parents, that she too was sent away to convent school, that she also subsequently lived in Montreal and Paris, and now lives, as Laura does, with her family in an Anglophone milieu in Toronto.

Clearly, Laura resembles Lola in more than fictional ways. But Tostevin does more than present a fictional cover for an autobiographical narrative. She constructs a questionable fiction towards the end of Laura's account of her life in "Le Baiser de Juan-les-Pins," the story of a sexual incident with a taxi driver in Paris. Despite its title, it is written in English and presented as a story (fiction?) Laura first attempts to write in French but can only actually write (integrate in her life) in English. The doubleness of the larger narrative surrounding this story is further marked by the way in which Tostevin recounts Laura's convent-child life in the third person while the rest of the narrative, consisting of Laura's adult perspective, is written in the first person. The only exception to this is a passage about her told from Geoffrey, her husband's, point of view. In this passage Geoffrey reflects that "Laura is the only person he knows who looks upon stories, the telling of them, as part of reality" (69). This highlights what Laura herself is doing in her life-narrative and gives rise to the thought that if fiction reflects and refracts reality in telling ways, then fiction may be a significant aspect of autobiography.

Like the play between the factual and the fictitious, the play between first and third persons often marks this new approach to the writing of autobiography. First person suggests self-narration (that autobiographical pact again), the authority of the I conveying its particular view—at the risk of slant, of bias, the unassailable subjectivity of the self enshrined in its own drama. Third person suggests a perspective that is more external, evidential—what can be observed about another, what can be described out there on the stage of the text/world the character inhabits. Tostevin, however, reverses this. In her alternating third-person segments of the novel, we get interior experience, imagistic emotional landscapes recounted as if they were fact: "Once, during the Christmas concert, while she sings 'Mon beau sapin,' her silence fills the auditorium with a forest of northern pines, fresh snow, and the aroma of the her mother's *tourtières*" (16). The contrast between how this sentence begins and what it conveys embodies a certain tension, a poignancy that mimics the child's rigidity of body under the strictures of convent rule while it speaks of her imaginative flights as if they were the site, as they are, of her actual life.

Elizabeth Hay takes a different tack in her approach to the blur between autobiography and fiction / myth / legend. The cultural material for Hay's narratives is not spoken legend, as it is with Tostevin, but excerpts from documents of Canadian history—explorers' journals, travelogues, biographies, ethnographic records. These are interwoven with first-person notations from daily life, diarylike in the way they blur narrator and author, which stage Hay's idiosyncratic process of reflection on past and present, family and city, what being Canadian means in a national sense and what it means in a highly personal sense. The observations engendered by this process gradually create the emotional development of a narrative that is sometimes lyrical and sometimes documentary.

The voice of a homesick Canadian in America's most exciting and most deteriorated city is the voice of someone writing or talking to herself, touching the totems that will ground her spectral identity. As such it is an identity both personal and collective, both mundane and mythic, as Hay seeks to articulate what it means to be a Canadian woman living in New York in the late 1980s. "Canada's mythology is the mythology of not having one, of being inarticulate about our past" (100), she writes. "That tense area between saying nothing and saying something badly. Canadian: you know it's there but you can't put your finger on it" (103). In all this absence there is presence, the "loose web of connection" (96) she builds by weaving her way through cultural memory banks. Her captivity tales are the reverse of conventional ones: tales not of white settlers captured by Indians but homesick Inuit captives of Arctic explorers who bring them to New York for show, or tales of Canadian artists suffering a loss of identity under the captivating glare of American lights. "The disappointment Canadians feel in themselves," Hay notes, fusing the personal and collective. "And yet here we are, at the source of all the stories we could ever want to know" (151). In her hands these stories leap off the pages of musty documents to become the ground of her own ambivalent relationship to home. In a series of eight "Removes" or sections, she writes her way out of that imprisoning sense of being remote from where she is so that she can break through to mythic levels of who she is, a northern woman suffering the intense heat of New York city, a woman in a dark apartment with two small children, a woman who keeps the spirit of Cold alive by letting him "chew on the fleshy tips of her fingers" (105).

Like Tostevin, Hay works with story, in her case story derived from history that she strips of its prefix *hi-*, its stamp of high culture catalogued and collected, museum-dead. When she discovers tiny fragments, emotional shards of Emily Carr's life, or Glenn Gould's, or Hannah's (one of the early Inuit captives), she winds them into mythic levels of her own life story. Similar fragments, personal in their obsessiveness, mundane in their detail, yet the essential tesserae of larger patterns of our psychic lives, constitute all of us. They make us recognizable to ourselves by their very ficticity, that luminosity of an emotionally authentic telling that gives them immediacy, fictive or factual as they may be in other contexts.

In Hay's narrative, the crucial ambivalence its ficticity reveals has to do with leaving home and going home as equally vital necessities. This double relationship to home, this wanting both, might stand as a metaphor for a woman writer's relation to the cultural codes which have formed her and which she is in the process of deforming in the performance of a self on the stage of her text.

Victoria. Feb. 18. 95

last night's dream about "bad" mothers (uncaring &/or controlling mothers)
—the residue, i suspect, of reading so many mss. about childhood abuse
for Mona's chapbook contest [Mona Fertig's Mothertongue Press]—
woke up thinking how therapy, or the kind Bridget does, teaches women to
re-mother themselves when they had inadequate mothering as children

also that the mother-daughter relationship
can be so loaded because many mothers see mothering as a chance to
redeem their own inadequately mothered selves—this can mean actually
giving better mothering than they had (expecting more of their daughters
as a result?)—or it can mean mapping their own needs over the possibly
different needs of the child & so ending up mothering the child-ghost of
themselves rather than their actual daughters

re-reading Kathy's "Writing the Risk In . . . ," her recasting of (<u>the</u> sexual)
difference "through a dialogic relationship with the changing symbolization
of gender" has got me thinking about the changing symbolization of the
mother in a changing society:

for the mother-daughter course: ask them to ask their mothers how
they saw motherhood & mothering when they first began—how they
think their mothers' mothers (grandmothers) saw it—how my students
see it now—

crucial to look at how the symbolic mother functions, or as Kathy quotes
Cixous "the mother as metaphor": "that the best of herself be given to
woman by another woman for her to be able to love herself"

& the endless problem of fusion which gets in the way of "the sharing
of knowledge & desire <u>across</u> differences" (Teresa de Lauretis essay in
differences)

—that perhaps the mother-daughter
relationship is our first ground for experiencing difference with another
woman & the way it's negotiated determines our potential for future

empathy/solidarity with other women—that perhaps only through feminist insight (theory & conversation) can we repair the torturous push-&-pull of sameness & difference in our relationships, whether as lovers or as friends—

seeing through the family-blind: that as lovers we become family for each other, how this generates a push to conform to sameness (identity), to repress our differences for the sake of romantic fusion, just as our childhood families tried to repress differences for the sake of that 1950s ethos, "harmony," solidarity, "keeping the family together"— until finally it explodes!

~ ~ ~

Victoria. March 2. 95

Dear Sidney Matrix,

(what a wonderful nom de plume for a feminist (& is it, a nom de plume?)— as distinct from the name of the father as plume is feminine . . .)

I've been struggling for days trying to articulate some sort of proposal for my contribution to your anthology & am resorting finally to a letter. I know the area i want to work in but cannot crystallize it very well for you beforehand. Perhaps it's that i've been completing the semi-final draft of a novel [Taken] & can't seem to shift very quickly from novelistic into theoretical gear. Or it's the same problem as coming up with a project description for a writing grant—the before-hand—since writing seems to require of me some working in the dark.

So, what i'm proposing to do is something rather fragmentary, inspired in part by DuPlessis' patchwork format in some of her HD work [Pink Guitar], something that allows me to shift easily between narrative/ anecdote & theory & journal entry. The theory will relate to an area i've been investigating for some time now, mother-daughter relationships, particularly fraught when the daughter is lesbian & the mother committed to self-definition through conventional notions of femininity. But since the novel i've been working on is semi-autobiographical, i want to write reflexively about the writing of autobiography, the kind of memory work involved in it, how that is intercut with a narrating present which recontextualizes constantly.

I'm sorry i can't be more explicit than this. Could be, once it's done!

~ ~ ~

Victoria. Apr. 20. 95

to write about the painful relationship with our mothers who were neither feminist nor lesbian, who have denied us (there's that "we" again)—

how we both long for & don't belong in the family—create new "families" of sisters but not mothers/daughters though we are constantly learning how to heal the damage of that first desirous relationship—the dangerous one (hence the primacy of sisterhood as our model for relating?)

"ghost stories" that continue to haunt: our mothers' unlived desires for themselves, who they might have been (desires which were <u>not</u> necessarily lesbian)—the lost chances, faint hopes—how hard it is to see the "other life" of one's mother as a woman of her time: the sense of history required, of stepping outside of our own in order to see it

Victoria. June 2. 95

writing as that which moves between self & other—as the erotic does (the pull of lesbian desire: the different in the "same")—tho the erotic, once lit, moves into a space where self & other, same & different, disappear sunburst in the mouth // sunrise dishes (NOT an equation // a bridge, a connection?)

haunting connection: mother-residue (in the dishes), or what is haunting is her ideal (self), the ideal she fosters (of an ideal daughter!) in the feminine—difficult to root out since mother as first love object = first model of how to be female

that sense of lack (-lustre self), passed on, leads to the struggle to be at home: to like one's self as a woman/lesbian (undoing internalized misogyny, homophobia)

& more: understanding the relativity of self in relation to others—Indra's net, or "self" as a knot in a larger net of relations through which fire runs, fire of connection/compassion that "feeling-with": love, & nothing less

For the private reader: interplay in the public realm

Written in 1996 in response to a request from Sidney Matrix, the following offers yet another investigation of the reader-writer relationship, more specifically in the context of lesbian autobiography. It oscillates between prose poetry and theory, between the public and the private, between "you" reading and "i" writing. As a sort of theoretical epithalamion (literary tradition in the West credits Sappho as the first to write wedding songs), it allowed me to celebrate my relationship with a new "you," muse-figure, reader and life-partner, Bridget MacKenzie.

Sunday morning traffic in this byway of crooked streets interconnected. Mixed housing—apartment buildings, derelict old places untouched for years though still inhabited, anonymous new stucco, renovated cottages like this one and "heritage" brick or wood affairs—all of them crowded together with fences fading in the sun. Sound travels. Rock rolling by on four wheels. Guffaws of young guys across the way sustaining the ragged edge of last night's party. A dog whining in its small enclosure behind a bindweed fence. Someone yells at it, both man and dog hidden by what passes for privacy.

I could describe our back garden with none of this, just the flare of scarlet runner beans climbing and fading into the luminous hedge next door (emerald and gold euonymus), or the deep fuchsia colour of nicotiana that wavers outside my window, or the deck where our dog pants on his side in sun-dazzle while shadows from a giant pear lengthen toward him. Stillness and then breeze shift, perimeter blur. Unbounded interplay.

This sense of a lapse from the traffic, a space where fences drop away, fences or the kept-up roles and definitions property entails. Lapsing into that which is interwoven, indeterminate and spacious inside the fleeting traffic of patriarchy. A lesbian house. And you reading through the quiet hours of Sunday in bed.

~ ~ ~

To write is to oscillate in the space between self and other, to move out from inside that which is not yet even privately read/said through the already read/said that is public (published) and back again. This back-and-forth movement across boundaries is a sort of testing, even contesting perhaps, of the necessity of what is being written. Particularly when the writing seems most personal, most "inside," there is this drive to conjure a reader/reading on the "outside." As if the two might collaborate to answer questions that plague writing: what is this really about? and does it matter? and to whom?

A lesbian writer in some sense already writes from the outside because she is regularly given back images of herself that tell her she is outside the norm (sorry, benefits don't apply / queer partners not included). This makes "you" all the more crucial, for "you" signals a shared reading space where words, not just the words but their context, their particular view, are understood. View from *veue* (Old French), that final *e* indicating a feminine past participle: so, already there is a certain specificity of the field of vision.

Inside, she feels herself to be not only lesbian and poet, say—already an even further specificity begins to declare itself—but any number of other categories the complex of her life might be indexed into. Any reader (this reader, for instance) coming to a writer's words also brings her own complex into play. Reading through the field of her own associations she either resists or occupies "I." I-dentifying, she may map over the work a divergent set of personal associations, collapsing the author's into her own. "You" offers her a space to occupy in relation to the writer's ("private") content.

Lapsus of identity: a slide, a slip between two personals? Not "too" personal and yet enough so to connect. In writing, this is hypothetical ground, but it hovers there the way the image of a garden hovers just beyond the retaining wall of a street. How construct a way into it? (Metaphors, those cantilevered bridges where reader and writer connect.)

~ ~ ~

Last night in a dream, Warren (my first real poetry teacher), clearly still alive in memory, was talking to one of his university colleagues, or rather this colleague was talking to him. Though i could see both of them, i could hear only one side of the conversation: what Warren's still-living colleague was declaring about his new love, a younger man, and the poems he had written for him, how this unforeseen opening in himself had given him a new lease on life. He would outlive Warren by some years, he said. Still he had to consider his own eventual death, the chance that these poems would fall into the hands of family who would be terribly shocked. What was he to do, perhaps burn them? Not really such a final act, he thought, as the passion they spoke of would go on living in him.

Standing in another part of the dream, i was looking at a pink telephone slip in my hand, a message to call someone to organize a workshop for some conference, but i had delayed and the pink slip had grown, acquired a small folio of pink slips all apparently telephone messages though the reverse of each was covered with writing, some in red ink, with odd jottings, slanted lines, one set with a heart drawn through them, and i realized that what i held in my hand were this man's poems.

Describing the dream to you, i noted the erotic/poetic surfacing under the institutions of academia and family, gay identity surfacing from under apparent straight. But was that the whole story? you asked. True, there was another motif: what's on paper (what gets published, read) and what lives off the record.

~ ~ ~

Language and where we get it from. The peculiarly old resonance of "the whole story," as in "that's not . . ." (from whose point of view?) And did you say it or do i now conjure you saying it out of my own years-old store of resonant phrases? Hearing now the resonance of mother-speak and how it works in us, how deep, how it burbles up through the critical terms we overlay it with.

By the time i met contemporary poetry through Warren Tallman, i was already steeped in heterosexual versions of romantic love and spirit. Pound's "bride awaiting the god's touch." H.D. offered an altogether absorbing digression, if only between the lines in *Palimpsest*. In the early sixties little was known of H.D., lesbian novelist; she was occluded under H.D. Imagiste, as Pound had styled her. In the sixties, lesbian writing glimmered like a hidden garden for me. Like Her in the as-yet-to-be-released *HERmione*, i was both caught by and in flight from a mother who taught the formulae for femininity.

Not only taught the formulae but defined herself and would define me according to the rigidities of those conventions. Mother as first love and first source of love; mother as first model of how to be someone marked female.

~ ~ ~

What i remember is the smell of new cloth at the Chinese tailor's when she took me with her to wait while she tried on a half-made evening gown, adjustments, a sleeve to be lengthened, a bodice refitted. Yards of white gathered at her waist, the feel of the cloth, her showing me what the embroidery would look like in its scarlet exuberance. At six or seven, i was impatient with sewing and only had eyes for her in that creamy flowing, crepe de chine flowering like fresh gardenias round her feet. I thought her gorgeous, the tailor, squatting on the floor to pin up the hem as she stood on thin brown paper, properly deferential.

Bored after a while, steeped in the airlessness of the shop, the richness of its smells a batik layering, all the bolts of colour laid out to touch, faded smells of cooking from the back, but most of all the hot scratchy stillness as if the cloth itself were soaking up the air while they talked over what she wanted—endless it seemed—i stared out between blinds at the usual stream of shoppers, loiterers, hawkers. Gradually, everything slowed so that i saw the teacups on the sidewalk, a bowl of rice and not the syce-driven cars. Saw, for a long moment, a girl younger than me, hanging around the tea-stall across the way, called back by others but staring with that territorial rudeness i knew, staring between people and cars at me, the outsider in her father's (was it? her uncle's?) shop—while i, guardian of this gorgeous mother, just as rudely stared back.

~ ~ ~

There is what matters on a collective scale—you too, any you reading this predicament of being alive at this moment in history and knowing so little of the whole story—and there is what matters on the most personal scale—how close to our own unknowing can we get?

The suddenness of memory rising full-blown some forty years on, unlikely connection on an ordinary street. The confines of colonialism, its rigid window frame i was trained to gaze out of, and another i gazing back from the edges of her own view, positing something outside my particular context. In this glimpse, glimpse only, do i make up what she feels? How else do i know who she might be? In the writing / reading / re-membering that constitutes such glimpses, she alters me.

~ ~ ~

Perhaps this is a (revising) lesbian resistance to the already formulated? Experiencing what can't be, at least in the terms i was taught to perceive the world through: just as lesbian desire moves against the family edict (and towards the unspoken, unspeakable charm a certain woman exerts). First love that was off the map / record / all those 78 love songs of the fifties i would later hum the words to, dancing at sock-hops rapt in the greatest con. You could dance with your girlfriend, yes, but only when the boys didn't ask. I hadn't yet learned that writing invokes resistance as it articulates (gingerly) broken bits of public language.

~ ~ ~

As it invokes celebration: this ordinary/unordinary breakfast with its opulent yellows i offer you. Amber, even ochre, slices of Hawaiian papaya, skin greenish yellow against the Goldendawn plates that are remnant of my mother's good dishes. To use them every day, even for breakfast, is to celebrate the endurance of connection, even while giving a twist to an old song. So, setting crescent moons of orange papaya on English briar rose, at least Johnson Brothers version of it now some fifty years old—rambling rose, the wild kind.

Or, from another view, just old plates an old-fashioned colour salvaged from a sentimental decade. Mere background to papaya and lime wedges standing translucent in the now. This may be how you see them—?

But then, for you papaya doesn't blur into rose or Penang slide into Vancouver and now Victoria as narrative begins:—everything lost during the Japanese occupation, she started over again in the post-war shipping of English goods to the Orient, putting together a new home around her loves and then, a few years later, shipping all of it and us to a newer world with its own set of associations ("yellow rose of Texas" we would sing, glued to the radio).

"Starting over again" a phrase petalled deep in the roses of these plates, each day's sunrise i wake to miraculous after darkness, destruction. Offering you fresh papaya and lime as the unspoken drift of a story reloops its beginning, desirous to reach you emerging out of your own and other narrative to lift this fruit to your lips:

~ ~ ~

This crossing of boundaries. (Your lips absorbing papaya as my eyes read yours for that sunrise burst of flavour.) Though crossing implies that boundaries continue to exist—as in "we crossed the border today," through two sets of border guards, and we do still maintain our border guards. More like crossing a half-built bridge anchored on one side and stretching into open space: canti-lever. Into another genre. Altered i-dentity.

Bibliography

Allen, Paula Gunn. *The Sacred Hoop: Recovering the Feminine in American Indian Traditions.* Boston: Beacon Press, 1986.

Anzaldua, Gloria. *Borderlands/La Frontera: The New Mestiza.* San Francisco: Spinsters/Aunt Lute, 1987.

Atwood, Margaret. *Murder in the Dark.* Toronto: Coach House Press, 1983.

Bersianik, Louky. *Le pique-nique sur l'Acropole, Cahiers d'Ancyl.* Montreal: VLB Éditeur, 1979.

Blau DuPlessis, Rachel. "Family, Sexes, Psyche." *The Pink Guitar: Writing as Feminist Practice.* New York, London: Routledge, 1990. 20–40.

Brand, Dionne. *Chronicles of the Hostile Sun.* Toronto: Williams-Wallace, 1984.

Brandt, Di. *questions i asked my mother.* Winnipeg: Turnstone, 1987.

Briffault, Robert. *The Mothers: A Study of the Origins of Sentiments and Institutions.* London: G. Allen and Unwin, 1927.

Brossard, Nicole. *MAUVE.* Trans. Daphne Marlatt. Montreal: NBJ, 1985.

———— *Lovhers.* Trans. Barbara Godard. Montreal: Guernica Press, 1986.

————. "Tender Skin My Mind." Trans. Dympna Borowska. In Ann Dybikowski, Victoria Freeman, Daphne Marlatt, Barbara Pulling, Betsy Warland, eds. *In the Feminine: Women and Words/Les Femmes et les Mots Conference Proceedings 1983.* Edmonton: Longspoon Press, 1985. Reprinted as "Lesbians of Lore," in Nicole Brossard, *The Aerial Letter.* Trans. Marlene Wildeman. Toronto: The Women's Press, 1988. 180–83.

———— *The Aerial Letter.* Trans. Marlene Wildeman. Toronto: The Women's Press, 1988.

————. "Ultrasounds." Trans. Lucille Nelson. In Lou Robinson and Camille Norton, eds. *Resurgent: New Writing by Women.* Urbana and Chicago: University of Illinois Press, 1992. 20–32.

Burnett, Anne Pippin. *Three Archaic Poets: Archilochus, Alcaeus, Sappho.* London: Duckworth, 1983.

Buss, Helen. "Mother and Daughter Relationships in the Manawaka Works of Margaret Laurence." MA Thesis, University of Manitoba, 1981.

Cameron, Anne. *The Journey.* San Francisco: Spinsters/Aunt Lute Book Company, 1986.

————. *The Annie Poems.* Madeira Park: Harbour Publishing, 1987.

Cixous, Hélenè. "The Laugh of the Medusa." Trans. Keith Cohen and Paula Cohen. In Elaine Marks and Isabelle de Courtivron, eds. *New French Feminisms: An Anthology*. New York: Schocken Books, 1981. 245–64.

Clark, Mary E. *Ariadne's Thread: The Search for New Modes of Thinking*. Houndsmill, London: The MacMillan Press, 1989.

Creese, Gillian and Veronica Strong-Boag, eds. *British Columbia Reconsidered: Essays on Women*. Vancouver: Press Gang, 1992.

Davey, Frank. "Words and Stones in *How Hug a Stone*." *Line* 13 (spring 1989): 40–46.

de Lauretis, Teresa. "Desire in Narrative." *Alice Doesn't: Feminism, Semiotics, Cinema*. Bloomington: Indiana University Press, 1984. 103–57.

_____. "The Essence of the Triangle or, Taking the Risk of Essentialism Seriously: Feminist Theory in Italy, the US, and Britain." *differences: a Journal of Feminist Cultural Studies* I, 2 (Summer 1989): 3–37.

de Lotbinière-Harwood, Susanne. *Re-Belle et infidèle / The Body Bilingual*. Montreal and Toronto: Les éditions du remue-ménage/Women's Press, 1991.

Dinnerstein, Dorothy. *The Mermaid and The Minotaur: Sexual Arrangements and Human Malaise*. New York: Harper and Row, 1976.

Duras, Marguerite. Interviewed by Susan Husserl-Kapit. "An Interview with Marguerite Duras." *Signs: Journal of Women and Culture in Society* I, 2 (winter 1975): 423–34.

_____ and Xavière Gauthier. Trans. Katharine A. Jensen. *Woman to Woman*. Lincoln and London: University of Nebraska Press, 1987.

Fawcett, Brian. "Sexual Detective: For One Man the Sexual Revolution is Over." *The Vancouver Review* 7 (winter 1991–92): 20–24.

Fitzgerald, Judith. *Diary of Desire*. Windsor: Black Moss Press, 1987.

Gauthier, Xavière. "Is there such a thing as women's writing?" Trans. Marilyn A. August. In Elaine Marks and Isabelle de Courtivron, eds. *New French Feminisms*. New York: Schocken Books, 1981. 161–64.

Gilligan, Carol. *In a Different Voice: Psychological Theory and Women's Development*. Cambridge and London: Harvard University Press, 1982.

Godard, Barbara. "Transgressions." *Fireweed* 5/6 (Winter 1979–Spring 1980), 120–29.

_____, Kathy Mezei, Gail Scott, and Daphne Marlatt. "SP/ELLE: Spelling out the Reasons." *Tessera* 1/*Room of One's Own* 8, 4 (January 1984): 4–18.

————. "Ex-centriques, Eccentric, Avant-garde: Women and Modernism in the Literatures of Canada." *Tessera* 1/*Room of One's Own* VIII, 4 (January 1984): 57–75.

————. "The Language of Difference." *Canadian Forum* LXIV, 750 (June/July 1985): 44–46.

————, ed. *Collaboration in the Feminine: Writings on Women and Culture from Tessera.* Toronto: Second Story Press, 1994.

Grahn, Judy. *The Highest Apple: Sappho and the Lesbian Poetic Tradition.* San Francisco: Spinsters, Ink, 1985.

Harris, Claire. "Three poems." *Fireweed* 16 (spring 1983): 35–41.

Hay, Elizabeth. *Captivity Tales: Canadians in New York.* Vancouver: New Star Books, 1993.

Hawthorne, Nathaniel. *A Wonder-Book and Tanglewood Tales.* Boston and New York: Houghton Mifflin, 1951.

Hejinian, Lyn. "The Rejection of Closure." *Poetics Journal* 4 (May 1984): 134–43.

Hirsch, Marianne. *The Mother/Daughter Plot: Narrative, Psychoanalysis, Feminism.* Bloomington and Indianapolis: Indiana University Press, 1989.

Homans, Margaret. "Her Very Own Howl: The Ambiguities of Representation in Recent Women's Fiction." *Signs: Journal of Women in Culture and Society* 9 (Winter 1983): 186–205.

Hutcheon, Linda. "Incredulity Towards Metanarrative: Negotiating Postmodernism and Feminisms." *Tessera* 7 (Fall 1989): 39–44.

Jiles, Paulette. "In Search of the Picara: Notes for Women's Literary Liberation." *This Magazine* 1: 19 (December 1985): 31–35.

————. *Sitting in the Club Car Drinking Rum and Karma-Cola: An Etiquette for Ladies Crossing Canada by Train.* Winlaw: Polestar Press, 1986.

Johnson, Barbara. "My Monster/My Self." *A World of Difference.* Baltimore: Johns Hopkins University Press, 1987: 144–54.

Kamboureli, Smaro. *in the second person.* Edmonton: Longspoon Press, 1985.

————. "Theory: Beauty or Beast? Resistance to Theory in the Feminine." *Open Letter* VII, 8 (summer 1990): 5–26.

————. "'Seeking Shape. Seeking Meaning': An Interview" with Phyllis Webb. *West Coast Line* 6 (Winter 1991–92): 21–41.

Kemp, Penn. "Mama Physical." *(f.)Lip* I, 1 (March 1987): 6–8.

Kogawa, Joy. "Panel Two: Audience Discussion." *Telling It: Women and Language Across Cultures.* The Telling It Book Collective, eds. Vancouver: Press Gang, 1990

Koski, Raija, Kathleen Kells, and Louise Forsyth, eds. *Les Discours féminins dans la littérature postmoderne au Québéc.* San Franscisco: The Edwin Mellen Press, 1993.

Kristeva, Julia. *Desire in Language: A Semiotic Approach to Literature and Art.* Ed. Leon S. Roudiez. Trans. Thomas Gora, Alice Jardine, and Leon S. Roudiez. New York: Columbia University Press, 1980.

Lamy, Suzanne. *d'elles.* Montreal: L'Hexagone, 1979.

Lee, Sky. *Disappearing Moon Cafe.* Vancouver and Toronto: Douglas and McIntyre, 1990.

Lemire Tostevin, Lola. *Double Standards.* Edmonton: Longspoon Press, 1985.

_____. "Daphne Marlatt: Writing in the Space that is Her Mother's Face." *Line* 13 (spring 1989): 32–39.

_____. *Frog Moon.* Dunvegan: Cormorant Books, 1994.

Livesay, Dorothy. *The Self-Completing Tree.* Victoria: Press Porcepic, 1986.

Lorde, Audre. "Uses of the Erotic: The Erotic as Power." In *Sister Outsider.* Trumansburg: The Crossing Press, 1984. 53–59.

Mezei, Kathy. "Writing the Risk In, Risking the Writing." *Tessera* 10 (summer 1991): 13–21. Reprinted in Barbara Godard, ed. *Collaboration in the Feminine: Writings on Women and Culture from Tessera.* Toronto: Second Story Press, 1994. 237–45.

Miller, Nancy K. "Arachnologies: The Woman, The Text, and the Critic." *The Poetics of Gender,* Nancy K. Miller, ed. New York: Columbia University Press, 1986. 270–95.

_____. "Women's Autobiography in France: For a Dialectics of Identification." In Sally McConnell-Ginet, Ruth Borker and Nelly Furman, eds. New York: Praeger Publishers, 1980. 258–273. *Women and Language in Literature and Society.* Reprinted in revised form as "Writing Fictions: Women's Autobiography in France. " In her *Subject to Change: Reading Feminist Writing.* New York: Columbia University Press, 1988. 47–64.

_____. "Emphasis Added: Plots and Plausibilities in Women's Fiction." *Subject to Change: Reading Feminist Writing.* New York: Columbia University Press, 1988. 23–46.

Moers, Ellen. *Literary Women: The Great Writers.* Garden City: Anchor/Doubleday, 1977.

Morrison, Toni. "The Site of Memory." In *Inventing the Truth: The Art and Craft of Memoir*, ed. William Zinsser. Boston: Houghton Mifflin, 1987. 101–24.

Mouré, Erin. *Furious*. Toronto: House of Anansi, 1988.

Nichol, bp. *The Martyrology*, Book V. Toronto: The Coach House Press, 1982.

————. "Things I Don't Really Understand About Myself." *Open Letter* VI, 2–3 (summer-fall 1985): scattered in fragments throughout issue.

Ovid. *Metamorphoses*. Trans. Rolfe Humphries. Bloomington: Indiana University Press, 1964.

Papapostolou, J.A. *Crete*. Trans. Alexander Doumas. Athens: Clio Editions, 1981.

Philip, Marlene Nourbese. *She Tries Her Tongue, Her Silence Softly Breaks*. Charlottetown: Ragweed Press, 1989.

Potrebenko, Helen. *Walking Slow*. Vancouver: Lazara Publications, 1985.

————. *Life, Love and Unions*. Vancouver: Lazara Publications, 1987.

Rich, Adrienne. *On Lies, Secrets, and Silence: Selected Prose 1966–1978*. New York: W. W. Norton and Company, 1979.

Rogers, Linda. *Queens of the Next Hot Star*. Lantzville: Oolichan Books, 1981.

Rooke, Connie. "Getting into Heaven: An Interview with Diana Hartog, Paulette Jiles and Sharon Thesen." *The Malahat Review* 83 (summer 1982): 5–52.

Scheier, Libby. *Second Nature*. Toronto: Coach House Press, 1986.

Scott, Gail. "Shaping a Vehicle for Her Use." In Ann Dybikowski et al., eds. *In the Feminine: Women and Words/Les Femmes et les mots conference proceedings 1983*. Edmonton: Longspoon Press, 1985. Reprinted in revised form in her *Spaces Like Stairs*.

————. *Spaces Like Stairs*. Toronto: The Women's Press, 1989.

————. "Main Bride Remembers Halifax." In Lou Robinson and Camille Norton, eds. *Resurgent: New Writing by Women*. Urbana and Chicago: University of Illinois Press, 1992. 98–110.

Smart, Pat. "Our Two Cultures." *Canadian Forum* LXIV, 744 (December 1984): 14–19.

Smith, Sidonie. *A Poetics of Women's Autobiography: Marginality and the Fictions of Self-Representation*. Bloomington: Indiana University Press, 1987.

The Telling It Book Collective: Sky Lee, Lee Maracle, Daphne Marlatt, Betsy Warland. *Telling It: Women and Language Across Cultures*. Vancouver: Press Gang, 1990.

232

Théoret, France. *The Tangible Word*. Trans. Barbara Godard. Montreal: Guernica, 1991.

Thesen, Sharon. *The Beginning of the Long Dash*. Toronto: Coach House Press, 1987.

_____. "Why Women Won't Write: Literary Theory's Dark Shadow." *The Vancouver Review* 5 (Summer 1991): 14–16.

Thomas, Audrey. *Intertidal Life*. Toronto: Stoddart, General Publishing, 1984.

Wachtel, Eleanor. "An Interview with Audrey Thomas." *Room of One's Own* X, 3/4 (March 1986): 7–61.

Walker, Barbara. *The Woman's Encyclopedia of Myths and Secrets*. New York: Harper and Row, 1983.

Wallace, Bronwen. *Signs of the Former Tenant*. Ottawa: Oberon Press, 1983.

Warland, Betsy. *Serpent (w)rite*. Toronto: The Coach House Press, 1987.

_____ and Daphne Marlatt. "Reading and Writing Between the Lines." *Tessera* 5 (September 1988): 80–90.

_____. *Proper Deafinitions: Collected Theorograms*. Vancouver: Press Gang Publishers, 1990.

Warner, Lavinia and John Sandilands. *Women Beyond the Wire*. London: Michael Joseph, 1982.

Webb, Phyllis. *Water and Light*. Toronto: Coach House Press, 1984.

Wittig, Monique. *The Lesbian Body*. Trans. David Le Vay. Boston: Beacon Press, 1973.

Wolf, Christa. *The Reader and the Writer: Essays, Sketches, Memories*. Trans. Joan Becker. New York: Signet, 1977.

_____. *Patterns of Childhood*. Trans. Ursule Molinaro and Hedwig Rappolt. New York: Farrar, Straus & Giroux, 1980.

Woolf, Virginia. *Mrs. Dalloway*. 1925. London: Triad Grafton, 1976.

_____. *Orlando*. 1928. London: Granada, 1977.

Wunderlich, Hans Georg. *The Secret of Crete*. Trans. Richard Winston. Athens: Efstathiadis Group, 1983.

Zimmerman, Bonnie. "The Politics of Transliteration: Lesbian Personal Narratives." *Signs: Journal of Women in Culture and Society* IX, 4 (summer 1984): 663–682.

Titles in the Writer as Critic Series
edited by Smaro Kamboureli

V: Nothing But Brush Strokes:
Selected Prose
Phyllis Webb
ISBN 0-920897-89-4
$15.95 pb

IV: Canadian Literary Power
Frank Davey
ISBN 0-920897-57-6
$17.95 pb

III: In Visible Ink:
crypto-frictions
Aritha van Herk
ISBN 0-920897-07-X
$14.95 pb

II: Signature Event Cantext
Stephen Scobie
ISBN 0-920897-68-1
$12.95 pb

I: Imaginary Hand
George Bowering
ISBN 0-920897-52-5
$12.95 pb